My Life Purpose:
How to Discover God's Call

Jon Ashley

Parson's Porch Books
www.parsonsporchbooks.com

My Life Purpose: How to Discover God's Call
ISBN: Softcover 978-1-949888-40-9
Copyright © 2018 by Jon Ashley

All rights reserved. No part of this book may be reproduced or transmitted in any form or by any means, electronic or mechanical, including photocopying, recording, or by any information storage and retrieval system, without permission in writing from the publisher.

All Scripture quotations are from the:

New Living Translation (NLT), copyright © 1996, 2004, 2015, Tyndale House Foundation. Used with permission.

New International Version (NIV), copyright © 1973, 1978, 1984, 2011, Biblica. Used with permission.

English Standard Version (ESV), copyright 2008, Crossway Bibles, Used with permission.

Message, (MSG) copyright 2002, Eugene H. Peterson, NavPress, Used with permission.

Life Application Bible, (LASB), copyright 1996, Tyndale House Foundation, Used with permission.

Cover Credit: Paul Valla, Modern Worship Director and Media Specialist, The Presbyterian Church of Fremont, Nebraska.

A set of PowerPoint slides for this sermon series is available for download at www.parsonsporch.com.

Videos of these sermons being preached are available to view at www.presbyterianfremont.org/sermons.

Parson's Porch Books is an imprint of **Parson's Porch & Book Publishers** in Cleveland, Tennessee, which has double focus. We focus on the needs of creative writers who need a professional publisher to get their work to market, & we also focus on the needs of others by sharing our profits with those who struggle in poverty by meeting their basic needs of food, clothing, shelter and safety.

A Special Thanks
to the congregation of The Presbyterian Church, Fremont, Nebraska
who first heard these sermons preached,
and to my wife and partner in ministry, Jen,
who helps me hear God's Call.

Contents

Sermons Matter 7

What Is My Purpose? 9
   Ephesians 1:3-14

The Call to Follow 22
   Matthew 4:18-25

The Call to Faith 36
   Psalm 31:13-14, 23-24

The Call to Fellowship 49
   Acts 2:42-47

The Call to a Special Function 61
   Romans 12:3-8

The Call to Be Fruitful 73
   John 15:1-17

Your Unique Vocational Call 86
   Ephesians 4:1-16

A Hope-Filled Formula 98
   Romans 8:18-39

How to Discover God's Call 111
   John 10:1-10

Sermons Matter

Parson's Porch Books is delighted to present to you this series called Sermons Matter.

We believe that many of the best writers are pastors who take the role of preacher seriously. Week in, and week out, they exegete scripture, research material, write and deliver sermons in the context of the life of their particular congregation in their given community.

We further believe that sermons are extensions of Holy Scripture which need to be published beyond the manuscripts which are written for delivery each Sunday. Books serve as a vehicle for the sermon to continue to proclaim the Good News of the Morning to a broader audience.

In this book, Jon Ashley provides a series of sermons called, *My Life Purpose: How to Discover God's Call*, which is designed as a workbook for study and self-examination of God's call in one's life. Rev. Ashley is well versed in scripture and the art of proclaiming God's Good News.

We celebrate the wonderful occasion of the preaching event in Christian worship when the Pastor speaks, the People listen and the Work of the Church proceeds.

Take, Read, and Heed.

What Is My Purpose?
Part 1 of *My Life Purpose: How to Discover God's Call*

Ephesians 1:3-14

> <u>Focus Statement:</u> Your purpose is more about *who you are in Christ* than *what you do*.
>
> <u>Function Statement:</u> Passionately pursue the calling of Christ!

Scripture Reading Ephesians 1:3-14 (NLT)

³ All praise to God, the Father of our Lord Jesus Christ, who has blessed us with every spiritual blessing in the heavenly realms because we are united with Christ. ⁴ Even before he made the world, God loved us and chose us in Christ to be holy and without fault in his eyes. ⁵ God decided in advance to adopt us into his own family by bringing us to himself through Jesus Christ. This is what he wanted to do, and it gave him great pleasure. ⁶ So we praise God for the glorious grace he has poured out on us who belong to his dear Son. ⁷ He is so rich in kindness and grace that he purchased our freedom with the blood of his Son and forgave our sins. ⁸ He has showered his kindness on us, along with all wisdom and understanding.

⁹ God has now revealed to us his mysterious will regarding Christ—which is to fulfill his own good plan. ¹⁰ And this is the plan: At the right time he will bring everything together under the authority of Christ—everything in heaven and on earth. ¹¹ Furthermore, because we are united with Christ, we have received an inheritance from God, for he chose us in advance, and he makes everything work out according to his plan.

¹² God's purpose was that we Jews who were the first to trust in Christ would bring praise and glory to God. ¹³ And now you Gentiles have also heard the truth, the Good News that God saves you. And when you believed in Christ, he identified you as his own by giving you the Holy Spirit, whom he promised long ago. ¹⁴ The Spirit is God's guarantee that he will give us the inheritance he promised and that he has purchased us to be his own people. He did this, so we would praise and glorify him.

MESSAGE

Let's pray...
Heavenly Father, we pray that your Word would come alive in our hearts and minds today and give us insight into your purpose for our lives. Lord, give me your words to speak, for my words alone are empty apart from you. In Jesus' name, Amen.

There are times in our lives when

1. <u>We may wonder, "What is my purpose?"</u>

- We may think we have a pretty good idea,
  - and then events in our lives cause us to reconsider...
- We may find ourselves wondering, and waiting, and seeking direction...

I recently returned from a 90-day sabbatical... and during my time away,
- I thought a lot about this...
- I considered all that I've learned and experienced over the course of my life,
  - And I sought God's heart for who the Lord is calling me to be,
    - and what the Lord is calling me to do...
      - And one result of this season of reflection is this sermon series,
      - in which we are exploring what the Bible says
      - about how to discover your purpose...

So... What about you?

Do you ever wonder, "What is My Purpose?"
- "Who am I created to be and what am I called to do?"
- "For what purpose have I been placed on this earth?"

In Ephesians 1,
- there is one foundational truth
  - that I believe Paul would want us to ground our "sense of purpose" on...

And here it is:
- <u>Your purpose is more about **who you are IN CHRIST**</u>
  - <u>than about **what you do**</u>
  - You see, Paul used the phrase "in Christ" (or one like it) **12 times** in these 12 verses,
    - and he speaks directly about our call, as believers, to spiritual union "in Christ" ...
  - And so, this morning, as we begin this new sermon series,
    - Let's explore what Paul says about WHO WE ARE IN CHRIST,
      - So that we may be better equipped to discover WHAT God is calling us to do

Sound like a plan?

My Life Purpose

Here we go ~
- Paul opens in verse 3,

  "All praise to God, the Father of our Lord Jesus Christ,

  *who has **blessed us with every spiritual blessing in the heavenly realms***

  *BECAUSE **we are united with Christ**."*

Isn't that awesome?!

2. <u>Your God-given purpose is:</u>
   - First,<u> to be **blessed** and **united** with Christ (v. 3)</u>
     - Think about that...
       ○ Your Heavenly Father's purpose is to BLESS you,
       ○ because the Lord has chosen YOU to be ONE with Jesus...

This summer, our family moved two of our girls to college in Arizona
- First Mikaela, who is now a senior at Grand Canyon University,
- And then Molly, who is just starting her freshman year at GCU

I remember three years ago, when we moved Mikaela into her first dorm room,
- And it was finally time to say goodbye, we were all in tears
  - It was such a change to no longer have Mikaela with us
- And so, while we were a little more prepared this time with Molly
  - (for we knew what to expect),
  - The transition was still difficult,
  - and it seems so weird to not have her at home with us now...

But... we also know it is good ~
- For part of our purpose as parents is to prepare and equip and bless our children
  - to be able to spread their wings – and fly
- And Mikaela has done that over these last 3 years,
  - And she is thriving in school, and in her work,
  - and I have no doubt God has a special purpose and plan for her life
- And now we are also able to see Molly grow into her future self

- And what a joy it is to be a part of blessing her with opportunities to learn and grow
- And even though they go to school 1339 miles away,
  - We are still united with them as one family
  - And even more, we know they are blessed by our Heavenly Father
    - with every spiritual blessing in the heavenly realms
    - because we are united with Christ!
- And I am encouraged, when I consider,
  - That all the love that I have for them as their earthly Father,
    - is but a small reflection of the *enormity* of Our Heavenly Father's love for them
  - And while the bond that Jen and I feel with our four daughters is strong and real,
    - Our union in Christ is even stronger ~
  - And so, what a joy it is to know our children are blessed and united with us in Christ,
    - And that *this is* God's purpose for our lives!

In verse 4, Paul adds:

"*Even before he made the world,* **God loved us** *and* **chose us IN CHRIST** *to be* **holy** *and* **without fault** *in his eyes."*

The NIV translation says we are "holy and blameless" in God's sight ~

I wonder... How many of you feel "holy and blameless" today?
- When you think about the thoughts you think,
- the decisions you make,
- and the actions you take,
- do you feel "holy and blameless"?

Well, that's how God sees you in Christ ~
- Your God-given purpose is <u>to be holy and blameless in God's sight</u>

The Message translation paraphrases God's purpose in verse 4 like this:

"*Long before he laid down earth's foundations,
he had us in mind, had settled on us as the focus of his love,
to be made whole and holy by his love.*"

You see, it's not because you are holy and perfect → that God chose you and loves you...

- (it's the other way around)
- Our salvation → is TOTALLY dependent → on God

The Life Application Bible describes it this way,
- "The mystery of salvation, originated in the timeless mind of God long before we existed
- It is hard to understand how God could accept us,
    - But because of Christ,
    - We are holy and blameless in his sight
- God chose us, and when we belong to him through Jesus Christ,
    - God looks at us as if we had never sinned
    - All we can do is express our thanks for his wonderful love!"

Paul continues to build on this idea in verse 5:
He writes, "**God decided in advance --** *to adopt us into his own family – by bringing us to himself through Jesus Christ. This is what he wanted to do, and it gave him great pleasure.*"

You see, God's purpose and pleasure is that you are
- <u>to be lovingly adopted into God's family</u> (v. 5)
    - Have you realized that?
        ○ God has chosen you to be His child
        ○ And to be a part of God's family...
    - It was God's choice – made in advance –
    - In his infinite love,
        ○ God has adopted us as his own children...

Now, the only real first-hand experience I have with adoption is with our pets
- And when I think about the relationship our family has with our dogs,
    ○ It is like they are part of our family...

We chose them...

- We love them... and we care for them...
- We experience companionship and unconditional love with them...
- Sometimes they drive us a little crazy,
- But they are part of our family...
    - And ever since a month ago, when we lost Jake, our black lab,
        - due to complications from surgery,
        - the feeling of loss in our family remains strong...
        - It's like part of us was taken away...
        - For we had lovingly "adopted" Jake into our family ~

And yet, when I think about how God must feel about His adopted children --

- How much greater is God's love for all of us?!?

For not only did God choose us,
- God also sacrificed his One and only Son,
    - For one purpose...

→ So that we would
- <u>be redeemed and forgiven by grace</u> (v. 6-7)

Paul wrote in verse 6 and 7,
"So, we praise God for the glorious grace he has poured out on us who belong to his dear Son. ⁷ He is so rich in kindness and grace that he purchased our freedom with the blood of his Son and forgave our sins."

Redemption... and Forgiveness... by Grace
- We could do a whole sermon series on this alone
    - But for now, let me say this...
        - **Our redemption is a gift from God,**
            - **purchased by the blood of Jesus**

You see,

- In Old Testament times,
  - Forgiveness was granted based on the shedding of animals' blood (Lev 17:11)

- Now, WE are forgiven based on the shedding of Jesus' blood ~
  - He died as the perfect and final loving sacrifice,
  - And as a result, we are forgiven and redeemed, by God's grace,
    - not because we've earned it,
    - but simply because of God's loving purpose and plan…

As a result,
- part of God's purpose for us,
  - is that we would <u>know the mystery of God's will</u>

- Paul writes in verse 9,

  "God has now revealed to us his mysterious will regarding Christ –

  which is to fulfill his own good plan"

And I don't know about you,
- But when I think about this truth ~
  - That God has chosen you and I to know the mystery of God's will…
  - It makes me feel special…
  - It's like God has clued us in on His Purpose for the World,
    - He's come along side us in Jesus Christ,
    - And revealed what He is up to
  - It's not a secret – it's the Good News of Jesus Christ!
    - And God has entrusted you and I with this message ~
      - And part of our purpose is to not only be aware and mindful of God's will,
      - But to pray for its fulfilment on earth,
      - And to work together to see God's purposes advanced…

For "at the right time", Paul adds in verse 10,

"(God) will bring everything together under the authority of Christ –
everything in heaven and on earth"
- We don't know when this day will come
  (Only God knows)
- But we do know that on that day,
   - when Jesus returns in power and glory,
   - and makes all things right and new,
   - that at that time, Jesus will be exalted to the highest place,
     (as Paul writes in Philippians 2)
   - "that at the name of Jesus every knee should bow,
       in heaven and on earth and under the earth,
        and every tongue declare that Jesus Christ is Lord,
      to the glory of God the Father." (Phil 2:10-11)

The exact timing of that Day remains a mystery ~
- But God has revealed his mysterious will and his plan to us
   - and in the meantime,
   - God has entrusted us with the opportunity and responsibility
     - to share the love and message of Jesus with others!

This is a vital aspect of our God-given purpose ~
- And when you accept it, by faith and trust in Christ,
- Paul adds in verse 13,
  Jesus "identifies you as his own,
      by giving you the Holy Spirit, whom he promised long ago"

And so, as a believer in Christ, your God-given purpose is also
- <u>to be sealed with the Holy Spirit</u> (v. 13)
  - The NRSV translation says you were "marked with the seal of the promised Holy Spirit"
    when you *heard* and *believed* in Jesus

This means God's Spirit lives in you!

My Life Purpose

- The Holy Spirit marks you as one who belongs to God!
- The Spirit seals your heart with the love and grace of God!
- The Spirit reveals God to and through you!
- The Spirit makes the power of Christ's sacrifice effective in your life!
- Through Christ, the Spirit makes you holy and blameless in God's loving eyes,
- And seals you forever, as belonging to God!

Imagine the story of your life being written in a book, authored by God,
- and before even one page is written,
- God places the seal of the Holy Spirit on each page,
- marking every moment,
    - every joy and sorrow,
    - every hill and valley,
    - every victory and every loss,
    - as part of Your story and God's story –
    - for the Spirit is *with you* and lives *within you* ~

Paul adds in verse 14,

*"The Spirit is **God's guarantee** that he will give us the inheritance he promised and that he has purchased us to be his own people."*

What an incredible, amazing gift this is!
- For the final chapter has already been written,
    - And we are God's people – who will inherit the riches of his glory!

(pause)

And yet, we still may wonder, WHY?
- Why has God done all this -- for us?
- Why has God filled each chapter of our lives with divine purpose,
- and sealed us with the Holy Spirit?

Perhaps, Paul's words in verse 12 and verse 14 give us a clue ~

- God has done all this, "so we would **praise** and **glorify** Him" ...

As the Westminster Confession of Faith puts it,
- The chief end of humankind "is to **glorify** God, and to **enjoy** him forever"

You see, God loves it when we **praise** Him!
- And we **glorify** God when we live according to His purposes ~
  - THAT's the Call of God on our lives!

Still, over the next few weeks,
- we will explore more of what the Bible says about the Call of God

Specifically, we will explore
3. Five Facets of God's Call ~
   - Including The Call to **Follow** Jesus...
   - The Call to **Faith**ful living...
   - The Call to **Fellowship** in genuine Christian community...
   - The Call to use our gifts in a special **Function**....
   - and the Call to be **Fruitful** for God ~

My hope and prayer is that as we explore these Five Facets of God's Call,
- Each one of us would become more aware of our personal Life Purpose,
  - No matter what age we are,
  - or what our background is ~
    - For I believe God has a special purpose and plan for each of us,
    - as well as for our life together...

Of course, in most cases, God's call becomes clearer over the course of time ~
- And the older we get, the stronger our sense of purpose may become...
- But certainly, it takes intentional effort and prayer to discover God's call for your life...
  - and I'm excited for the journey ahead of us...

I recently came across a list of life lessons, written over the course of one person's life

My Life Purpose

- And I'd like to share it with you,
    - as an example of how our sense of purpose grows over time...

Its titled, "Things Get Better with Age" by Jerry Lambert...

I've learned that I like my teacher because she cries when we sing "Silent Night." Age 5

I've learned that our dog doesn't want to eat my broccoli either. Age 7

I've learned that when I wave to people out in the country, they stop what they are doing and wave back. Age 9

I've learned that just when I get my room the way I like it, Mom makes me clean it up again. Age 12

I've learned that silent company is often more healing than words of advice. Age 24

I've learned that brushing my child's hair is one of life's great pleasures. Age 26

I've learned that wherever I go, the world's worst drivers have followed me there. Age 29

I've learned that if someone says something unkind about me, I must live so that no one will believe it. Age 30

I've learned that there are people who love you dearly but just don't know how to show it. Age 42

I've learned that you can make someone's day by simply sending them a little note. Age 44

I've learned that children and grandparents are natural allies. Age 47

I've learned that no matter what happens, or how bad it seems today, life does go on and it will be better tomorrow. Age 48

I've learned that singing "Amazing Grace" can lift my spirits for hours. Age 49

I've learned that you can tell a lot about a man by the way he handles these three things: a rainy day, lost luggage, and tangled Christmas tree lights. Age 51

I've learned that regardless of your relationship with your parents, you miss them terribly after they die. Age 53

I've learned that making a living is not the same thing as making a life. Age 58

I've learned that life sometimes gives you a second chance. Age 62

I've learned that if you pursue happiness, it will elude you. But if you focus on your family, the needs of others, your work, meeting new people, and doing the very best you can, happiness will find you. Age 65

I've learned that everyone can use a prayer. Age 72

I've learned that even when I have pains, I don't have to be one. Age 74

I've learned that every day you should reach out and touch someone. People love that human touch - holding hands, a warm hug, or just a friendly pat on the back. Age 76

(And finally,)

I've learned that I still have a lot to learn. Age 78

Friends, let's be purposeful and open to learning new ways that God is shaping us,

- as we <u>Passionately pursue the call of Christ</u> on our life journey!

Amen? Amen.

Let's pray...

Heavenly Father, we love you so much. And we pray that you would continue to shape us into the people you have created us and called us to be. May our lives bring praise and glory to You, O Lord. We pray this in Jesus' name, Amen.

REFLECT and RESPOND (Questions for personal or group reflection):

- Read today's Bible passage. How is the Holy Spirit speaking to you?

- In the past, how have you described the purpose of your life?

- How does it feel to know your life pleases God?

- Which of the God-given purposes above is most significant to you? Why?

- How will you praise and glorify God this week?

- How has your understanding of your life purpose grown today?

The Call to Follow

Part 2 of *My Life Purpose: How to Discover God's Call*

Matthew 4:18-25

> Focus Statement: Jesus calls us to follow him – the first step in discovering our life purpose.
>
> Function Statement: Decide to follow Jesus and discover your life purpose!

Scripture Reading   Matthew 4:18-25 (NLT)

¹⁸ One day as Jesus was walking along the shore of the Sea of Galilee, he saw two brothers—Simon, also called Peter, and Andrew—throwing a net into the water, for they fished for a living. ¹⁹ Jesus called out to them, "Come, follow me, and I will show you how to fish for people!" ²⁰ And they left their nets at once and followed him.

²¹ A little farther up the shore he saw two other brothers, James and John, sitting in a boat with their father, Zebedee, repairing their nets. And he called them to come, too. ²² They immediately followed him, leaving the boat and their father behind.

²³ Jesus traveled throughout the region of Galilee, teaching in the synagogues and announcing the Good News about the Kingdom. And he healed every kind of disease and illness. ²⁴ News about him spread as far as Syria, and people soon began bringing to him all who were sick. And whatever their sickness or disease, or if they were demon possessed or epileptic or paralyzed—he healed them all. ²⁵ Large crowds followed him wherever he went—people from Galilee, the Ten Towns, Jerusalem, from all over Judea, and from east of the Jordan River.

MESSAGE

Let's pray…
Heavenly Father, we love you, and we give thanks for the life of Jesus. Open our ears and our hearts to hear a message from you this morning. Lord, give me your words to speak, for my words alone can accomplish nothing apart from you. In Jesus' name we pray, Amen.

One of my earliest memories was of a fishing trip my Dad took me on ~

- I must have been around 4 or 5 years old,
- And he took me fishing on a lake in Nebraska
- I remember having such a good time with my father,
    - As he taught me how to put a worm on a hook, how to cast, and all…
    - and then acting so proud of me when I caught more fish than he did!
- When we got home,

- o My dad took a picture of me,
- o holding up a stringer full of fish...

So, when I became a father,

- I couldn't wait to teach our firstborn child how to fish ~
- We lived in California at the time (it was during seminary),
  - o And so, we drove up to a small lake near Big Bear.
- Only about four years old,
  - o Mikaela was the smallest person fishing on the lake...
  - o She had practiced casting at home with her bright green Tweety-bird fishing pole...
  - o And so, once we got the bait on her hook,
  - o She cast it out – about 50 feet into the lake...
- And within a matter of seconds,
  - o A fish struck,
  - o And her line went tight ~
    - "You got one!"
    - "Reel it in! Reel it in!"
  - o Reaching around her from behind,
    - I helped her reel in the first catch of her young life...
      - A 3-pound Rainbow Trout!
  - o "Wow! Look at that!", I said, in utter amazement ~
    - "So how do you like fishing?!"

- With eyes wide open in wonder,
  - o She burst out, "I'm so excited - my bum is shaking!"

Here's a photo that we took the next day after we got home...

I love fishing...

And while my Father taught me how to fish,

- And I've taught all four of our daughters how to fish,
- There is perhaps nothing as rewarding as fishing *for souls...*

"Come, follow me", Jesus said, "and I will show you how to fish for people."

In chapter 4 of his Gospel, Matthew describes a Fishing Story
- And it all starts with The Call to Follow

Now, if you were here last week,
- You may recall that we introduced the <u>Five Facets of God's Call</u> ~
    1) The Call to Follow
    2) The Call to Faith
    3) The Call to Fellowship
    4) The Call to a Special Function, and
    5) The Call to be Fruitful

And our focus today, is on the **first Facet** of God's Call:
4. <u>The Call to Follow</u>
    - You see,
        - I may have never learned how to fish if I hadn't followed my dad's lead...
        - And our girls may have never learned if they hadn't followed me...

And so, if we want to discover God's Purpose for our lives,
- The first step is to answer the call to follow Jesus ~

In verse 18 and 21,
- <u>Jesus invited two sets of brothers to follow Him</u> (v. 18, 21)
    - First, there was Simon and Andrew...
        ○ and then James and John...

    - All four of them were professional fishermen,
        ○ So, they weren't just fishing for fun or leisure ~
            - they were hard at work,
            - casting their commercial fishing nets into the Sea of Galilee...

And yet, as Jesus walked by and saw them,
- he called to them,
  - And <u>He promised to give them a **new purpose**</u> (v. 19)
    - They would no longer merely cast fishing nets for a living ~
    - True living would now involve casting nets of love – to capture hearts and minds ~
    - Jesus called them to follow Him,
      - And **he would teach them how to fish -- for people...**

As for the four brothers,
- <u>they left their old life -- and followed Jesus</u> (v. 20, 22)
  - Verse 20 says Simon Peter and Andrew left their nets "at once" and followed him
  - And verse 22 says James and John not only left their boat,
    - *They left their father behind* as well, and immediately followed Jesus...

Now, it's important to note here that
- these four were average men – not the bravest or easiest to work with...
  - they weren't highly qualified when it came to people skills...
    - Simon Peter was impulsive and headstrong...
    - Andrew was down-to-earth and supportive...
    - James and John were ambitious and called "Sons of Thunder" ...
  - And yet, **all four of them were willing to change,**
    - to identify with Christ and his mission,
    - and become partners with Jesus in ministry...

And as a result,
- As they traveled throughout the region of Galilee with Jesus,
- They cast a wide net,
- <u>And many more people heard the Good News</u> ~
  - Jesus taught in the synagogues,
    - and announced the Good News of the Kingdom of God
      - He taught his disciples the power of God's Word to transform hearts,
      - And he continued to preach truth to all who would listen...

- The disciples, of course, probably formed a Worship Committee,
    - a Fellowship Committee,
    - and a Community Outreach Committee (among others) ...

Clearly,

- They developed a social media strategy and prepared for a medical mission program
    - And in time, news about Jesus spread as far Syria,
    - and people started bringing their sick friends and relatives to Jesus...

Of course, it didn't matter to Jesus what their disease or ailment was ~

- <u>He healed them all</u> (v. 24)
    - Whether they were suffering spiritual attacks, mental illness, or physical sickness,
        - Jesus healed them ~
            - He healed their bodies,
            - their hearts,
            - their minds,
            - and their souls...

    - And through it all,
        - He was showing the disciples how to fish for people:
            - 1) Meet real needs,
            - 2) Share the Good News, and
            - 3) And welcome people to join in following Jesus

It's no surprise then,

- <u>That large crowds followed Jesus</u> wherever he went (v. 25)
    - People from near and far came to Jesus and found **healing**, **purpose** and **hope** ~
        - In fact, in the next three chapters of Matthew,
            - Jesus gave the Sermon on the Mount,
            - and then continued to perform miracles and healings,
            - all the while teaching his disciples more and more about how to fish for people...

- Finally, in Matthew chapter 10,
  - Jesus called his twelve disciples together and gave *THEM* the authority
    - to cast out evil spirits,
    - heal the sick,
    - announce the coming of the Kingdom of Heaven,
    - and even raise the dead!

- And the disciples joined Jesus on **His Fishing Mission** –
  - to save and restore lost souls!

As many of you know,
- in June, our church sent 30 youth and adults on a mission trip to Puerto Rico,
- and while we did a lot of home repairs,
  - gave away water filtration systems,
  - and cleaned up debris from the Hurricane…
- We also listened to people's stories,
  - and prayed with many of them to overcome loss and worry and fear,
- As we worked to meet real needs,
  - we sought to offer hope and share the love of Jesus…

In many ways,
- We learned and experienced how to "fish for people" ~
  - and we saw the Lord change lives before our very eyes ~

One of the most profound transformations we witnessed was a man named Jimmy,
- His neighbor shared with us,
  - That ever since the hurricane,
  - Jimmy struggled with depression and severe alcoholism…
- So, for 3 days, we prayed for Jimmy outside his severely damaged home
  - before we finally met him one morning,
    - as he was stumbling home from the neighborhood bar

- And when we were able to listen to his story,
    - And offer a word of hope and encouragement,
        - He broke down in tears and embraced us as we prayed with him ~
            - We prayed for healing and strength...
            - We prayed for the power to overcome fear...
            - We prayed that Jimmy's life would glorify God...
            - and that God would work through him to be a light for others...

And after our time of prayer,
- You could see a visible change on Jimmy's face ~
    - From a drunken look of despair and hopelessness,
        - → to a glowing smile of joy -- and purpose -- and hope for his future ~
            - He then surprised us, as he literally stomped on his mostly-full can of beer, (which exploded and sprayed all over us!)
    - But if you think about it,
        - Smashing that can was like "dropping his net",
            - and choosing a new way to live ~
        - It symbolized Jimmy leaving his old life behind,
            - and following his new-found purpose in Christ!

Like Simon, Andrew, James and John,
- Jimmy started a new journey with Jesus ~
    - One that would be filled with ups and downs -- joys and challenges,
    - But one that was also now filled with hope and purpose!

Isn't God awesome?!

Because if you think about – all this was made possible because months earlier,
    (and for seven years now)
- Our church made and sold Apple and Cherry pies to raise funds for mission trips...

And when we prayed about the opportunity to go and serve in Puerto Rico,

- 30 people heard God's call –
  - and made the choice to **follow Jesus** ~
  - We sought to reach out with God's love,
  - and the Lord changed lives – including Jimmy and many others,
    - and along the way, our lives were changed as well!

This was God's purpose all along ~ to change lives ~

- **But it all started because people chose to answer the call to follow ~**

The same can be said of Simon Peter ~
- His life was completely transformed by Jesus ~
  - From a bold and boisterous professional fisherman,
    - to the Apostle appointed to lead the Church in Jerusalem…

But it wasn't always smooth sailing,
- in fact, Simon Peter stumbled on numerous occasions ~
  - missing the point of many parables…
  - reprimanding Jesus and then having the Lord respond, "Get away from me, Satan!"
  - resorting to violence in the Garden of Gethsemane,
  - and denying Jesus as predicted – not once, not twice, but three times…

Yet, through it all, Jesus never gave up on him ~
- Instead, He walked with his imperfect disciple,
  - and taught him how to fish for people…

And so, let's consider
5. <u>The Case of Simon</u> – and see how the "Five Facets of God's Call" played out in his life,
   - And how his example -- and experience -- may speak into our lives as well…

First, when the Lord said, "Come, follow me",
- <u>Simon decided to follow Jesus</u>

- He could have ignored Him ~
- But instead, he dropped his fishing net and made a choice to follow God's call
- He said "Yes" to the Lord's invitation…

But I wonder… what if you were in his shoes?
- How would you have responded to Jesus?

Think about it -- if Jesus walked into your place of work,
- or into your home or school,
- and called you to follow him,
  - how would you respond?

Even more…
- Have you listened for the Call of God in your life?
- Or have you been too distracted with other things?
- How have you responded to Christ's Call to follow Him?
- Have you let go of other competing priorities?
- Have you decided to follow Jesus, however He may lead you?

For Simon, the transformation was more of a ***process*** than an instantaneous change ~
- Over time, He learned to trust Jesus ~
  - He answered the Call to Faith (the 2nd Facet of God's Call) ~
  - By watching, and listening…
    - and learning from the Lord…
  - He believed in his heart,
    - and verbalized his faith with his lips
  - He trusted Christ as The Promised "Messiah,
    - the Son of the living God" (Mt 16:16)
  - And as he learned to trust in Jesus,
    - His life was transformed from a plain fisherman,
    - To a new person with new goals and new priorities…

My Life Purpose

What about you?

- How would you describe your relationship with Jesus?
  - Do you trust Him?
    - How has your trust grown over time?
    - What difference has your faith in Christ made in your life?
      (BTW - The Call to Faith will be our focus next week, and I hope you'll be here!)

For Simon Peter, one of the greatest changes that unfolded on his faith journey was

- <u>His experience of true Christian fellowship</u> (the 3rd Facet of God's Call) ~
  - It was like he had a new family ~
    - Brothers and sisters in Christ, whom he loved deeply
  - He grew to become one of the inner-circle of disciples who was closest to Jesus,
    - and the bond of brotherly love among them was genuine and real ~

  - Have you experienced the joy of authentic Christian fellowship?
    - Do you have brothers and sisters in Christ who are like family to you? ~
      - You know you can turn to them for help in a time of need,
      - And you support one another with prayer and loving concern?

This week, a group of 14 or so men went on our Annual Niobrara Man Trip

  (I went up Thursday, and came back yesterday)

- And while we had tons of fun camping, and hunting and fishing and stuff,
- The best times were the campfire talks and devotional times,
  - which focused on Romans 12:9-13, where Paul writes,

  "Don't just pretend to love others. Really love them. Hate what is wrong. Hold tightly to what is good. Love each other with genuine affection,[a] and take delight in honoring each other. Never be lazy but work hard and serve the Lord enthusiastically. Rejoice in our confident hope. Be patient in trouble and keep on praying. When God's people are in need, be ready to help them. Always be eager to practice hospitality." (NLT)

And you know what was cool?!

- We *experienced* the type of genuine Christian fellowship that Paul describes ~

My Life Purpose

- We loved each other with genuine affection…
- He honored one another…
- We served the Lord enthusiastically…
- And yesterday, when one of us shared a personal struggle,
    - the whole group gathered around him,
    - laid hands on him,
    - and prayed for our brother in Christ…
        - it was so powerful and awesome to experience…

Church -- the Call to true Christian Fellowship is open to all of us ~

- and like Simon Peter and the disciples,
- we all can engage with others in purposeful ways…

The question is…

- Will you answer the call?
- Will you seek out purposeful relationships with others in God's family?

Simon did just that ~

- He acted on the Call to Follow…
- He grew in the Call to Faith…
- He experienced the Call to true Christian Fellowship…
- And fourthly, <u>he used his God-given gifts</u> in service to God and others…

For example,
- His *passionate faith* and *boldness*
    - helped him lead others to Jesus…
- His *courage* and *compassion*
    - made him the first great voice of the gospel during and after Pentecost…
- And his *giant heart* and *hard work*
    - helped to serve and grow the church for years to come…

Jesus saw all these gifts in Him,

- And Jesus saw the great potential of what God could do in his life ~

So, some 12 chapters later, in Matthew 16,
- Jesus spoke a new purpose into his disciple's life ~

    > "Now I say to you, that you are Peter (which means 'rock'), and upon this rock I will build my church, and all the powers of hell will not conquer it.
    > And I will give you the keys of the Kingdom of Heaven."

And so, you see,
- In God's time,
- <u>Simon became Peter -- "The Rock" and foundation of The Church</u> (16:18)
    - Jesus called Peter to a new purpose – to teach others how to fish for people ~
    - and countless lives were changed through him ~
        - as he preached about Jesus,
        - and shared his life and faith and gifts in Christian community...
    - It was not an overnight transformation ~
        - In fact, his new purpose and identity in Christ
            - was not fully realize until after the resurrection of Jesus ~
        - **But none of it would have happened,**
            - **if he hadn't answered the Call to Follow...**

And that's where it starts for you and me, too ~
- When we "drop our nets" and leave our old way of living behind,
    - and then Follow Jesus...
- When we learn to grow in a trusting faith relationship with our Lord,
    - and engage in true Christian fellowship with one another...
- When we use our God-given gifts for good – to grow the Kingdom,
- When we do all of this, our lives become purposeful and fruitful...
(the 5th Facet of God's Call)

So, I urge you – <u>Decide to follow Jesus -- and discover your life purpose!</u>
- to God be the Glory, Now and Forever!

My Life Purpose

Let's pray... Heavenly Father, you spoke – and the disciples followed. You proclaimed the Good News – and people were healed. In the same Spirit, you call us to follow Jesus, and you give our lives renewed purpose and hope. And so today, we accept your invitation. Come into our hearts and make us new inside. Heal us. And transform us into the people you are calling us to become. We pray this in Jesus' name, Amen.

REFLECT and RESPOND (Questions for personal or group reflection):

- Read today's Bible passage. How is the Holy Spirit speaking to you?

- Why do you think Peter, Andrew, James and John responded to Jesus as they did?

- What promise did Jesus offer them?

- How would you have responded to Jesus? How are you responding?

- What was the impact of the disciples' decision to follow Jesus?

- How has following Jesus changed your life?

The Call to Faith
Part 3 of *My Life Purpose: How to Discover God's Call*

Psalm 31:13-14, 23-24

> Focus Statement: The call to faith is a call to trust and depend on God.
>
> Function Statement: Be strong and courageous as you trust in Christ!

Scripture Reading   Psalm 31:13-14, 23-24 (NLT)

*¹³ I have heard the many rumors about me,
    and I am surrounded by terror.
My enemies conspire against me,
    plotting to take my life.
¹⁴ But I am trusting you, O LORD,
    saying, "You are my God!"*

*²³ Love the LORD, all you godly ones!
    For the LORD protects those who are loyal to him,
    but he harshly punishes the arrogant.
²⁴ So be strong and courageous,
    all you who put your hope in the LORD!*

MESSAGE

Let's pray...
Heavenly Father, your Word gives hope to our hearts. Make it come alive in us this morning, that we might grow in faith and love, through the work of the Holy Spirit. In Jesus' name, Amen.

Nine-year-old Joey was asked by his mother what he had learned at Sunday school.

"Well, Mom,
- our teacher told us how God sent David -- the smallest of shepherd boys –
- on a secret mission behind enemy lines to take down Giant Goliath – an evil foreign agent!

My Life Purpose

As David approached, he used a laser sight to pinpoint the coordinates of his target,
- then radioed in to headquarters on his walkie-talkie to order a drone strike!

Within moments, Goliath was vaporized –
- making David a War Hero, who was promoted to King of Israel,
- and who became an ancestor in the family tree of Jesus Christ."

"Now, Joey, is that really what your teacher taught you?" his mother asked.

"Well, no… **But if I told it the way the teacher did, you'd never believe it!"**

Today we are exploring the "Call to Faith" ~
- And while there are many examples throughout the Bible of people who lived by faith,
- We're going to look specifically today at

<u>The Life and Faith of David</u>

Of course,
- David is most well-known for his against-all-odds defeat of Goliath in battle,
  - armed with nothing more than a stone-throwing sling
- The story of David and Goliath is a classic favorite ~
  - It's a story of an underdog defeating a mighty giant…
  - It's a story of good conquering over evil…
  - It's a story of faith overcoming fear…

But immediately after David killed Goliath,
- and the inspired Israelite army wiped out the intimidated Philistine army,
  - David was introduced to King Saul and his son, Jonathan ~
    - and David and Jonathan became instant BFF's ~
  - But King Saul was a jealous, insecure man,
    - and before long, he resented David's growing success and popularity,
    - and tried to kill him multiple times!

My Life Purpose

Whether it was Saul repeatedly throwing his spear at David in a fit of rage,
- or sending David back out into battle hoping he'd be killed by the Philistines,
- <u>David was hated and threatened by his enemies</u> (v. 13)
    - Saul and his servants planned to assassinate David,
        - but Jonathan warned him, and David escaped…
    - Saul sent troops to kill David,
        - But David's wife, Michal (Saul's daughter), helped him escape
    - This routine continued over and over ~
        - with Saul and other enemies chasing David all over, trying to kill him,
            - but with David narrowly escaping every time,
            - by God's grace…

    - So, when we read Psalm 31 verse 13,
        - we can sense the stress in David's tone:

        "I have heard the many rumors about me,
            and I am surrounded by terror.
        My enemies conspire against me,
            plotting to take my life."

Eventually, in God's time,
- Saul himself was hunted down by the Philistines,
    - and after his death, and the death of his son, Jonathan,
    - David became the new King ~
        - But his troubles didn't end there ~

In fact, after restoring the nation to peace and great military power,
- David's personal life became entangled in sin:
    - He committed adultery with Bathsheba…
        - and then ordered her husband (Uriah) killed in an attempted cover-up…
    - It was like *General Hospital* ~
        - meets *Criminal Minds*…
        - meets *Scandal*…

Yet, through it all,

<u>And despite his failures,</u>

- David chose to **fully trust** in God
    - No matter how stressful and fearful his life became,
        - He was "all in" with God, all the way...

    - His enemies may have been out to get him,
        - His decisions and actions may have been catching up to him,
        - and the pressures of his position may have been weighing heavily on him,
        - "But", as he added in verse 14,

        "I am trusting you, O LORD,
        saying, 'You are my God!'"

And you know what?

- God loves to hear that from us! ~

    "No matter how bad things get, God..."
    "No matter how many times I fail and make a mess of my life..."
    "I AM **TRUSTING** YOU, O LORD ~"
    "YOU ARE **MY** GOD!"

That's what The Call to Faith is all about ~

- Trusting in God, no matter what ~
    - Faith is not just about coming to believe, or accept something as true ~
        - It's not just about mental assent to "facts" or "head knowledge" ...
    - It's about TRUSTING GOD in your heart ~
        - It's about RELYING and DEPENDING on the Lord,
            - because GOD is FAITHFUL and TRUSTWORTHY!

For David, he experienced the faithfulness of God in a very personal way ~

- For the Lord protected him –
    - and blessed him –
        - over and over again ~

- And along the way,
  - through all the ups and downs,
  - <u>David was supported in godly fellowship</u> by those who joined him on the journey
    - In fact, many times, when he was seemingly at the end of his rope,
      - he would receive unexpected help from a loved one ~
      - as if the Lord were intervening to offer support, care, and guidance...

For sure, the gift of David's friendship with Jonathan was special ~

- And their close bond literally saved David's life on numerous occasions...
  - David personally experienced the power of God's love,
    - in fellowship with friends and family alike ~

  - And it was through such relationships
    - that David lived out his faith in community with others ~
      - worshipping,
      - working,
      - and serving the Lord ~

  - It was with this heart of worship that David urges us in verse 23,

    "Love the Lord, all you godly ones!"

    "For God takes care of all who stay close to him!"

    You see,

    David witnessed the power of God
    - to give victory over his enemies,
  - and he received comfort and peace from the Lord
    - in times of loss and despair...

...But at the same time,
- his life was far from easy ~
- For <u>David also suffered the consequences of his disobedience</u>

- As he added in verse 23,

    Yes, "...the Lord protects those who are loyal to him,

    "but he harshly punishes the arrogant."

Of course, David experienced God's punishment first hand in his life

- For there were times when his pride and arrogance became an obstacle in his faith
    - and he suffered the consequences...

- Specifically,
    - The Lord told David directly,
    - that because of his unfaithfulness,
        - the child he had with Bathsheba would die as punishment,
        - and his entire household would rebel against him...

Still,

- <u>David's love of God never wavered</u> (v. 24; 1 Sam 13:14)
    - On the day his unnamed child with Bathsheba died,
        - David didn't walk away from God in anger and bitterness...
        - He didn't try to escape his pain through more sinful indulgence ~

    - Instead,
        - David got up from the ground,
            - Got cleaned up and dressed,
            - and went to the Tabernacle and worshiped the Lord

    - Even through all the pain and suffering of his loss,
        - David's love of God never changed ~
            - He continued to trust and depend on the Lord through it all
            - For as Samuel described him,
            - David was "a man after God's own heart"
        - And he answered the Call to Faith
            - with a constant outlook of trust and dependence toward God...

Last Sunday was World Communion Sunday,

- And in addition to sharing the Lord's Supper here together in worship,
  - I had the joy of taking Communion to several members of our church family
    - who are homebound or living in Care Centers,
  - And in doing so,
    - I witnessed the living faith of some of our church family,
      - who put their hope in the Lord ~?

One such person is Sandy,
- She is currently undergoing physical rehabilitation at Life Care Center in Elkhorn,
  - after falling in her home and breaking her hip in early September
- In addition,
  - Before that, Sandy had to have one of her legs amputated,
    - and she requires dialysis three days a week...

She's been through the ringer ~
- But you would never know it, visiting her ~
  - She has answered the Call to Faith with a daily trust and dependence on God
  - And if you know Sandy, you know she has a heart for people ~
    - And she loves helping others and making them feel special

Now,
- Some people who have suffered as many setbacks and challenges as Sandy
  - may become understandably bitter and feel sorry for themselves...
- But not Sandy ~ her struggles seem to have made her stronger,
  - and She is making the most of her situation ~

For example,
- as we were going down the hallway toward the dining hall to share communion, we passed a man named Robert,
  - and Sandy said, "Robert, would you please sing Pastor a song?"
- Robert proceeded to belt out a beautiful love song, with vigor and vibrato,
  - and when he finished, everyone in the hallway applauded

- - and his face lit up,
  - as if he were living out his life purpose ~

  - After Sandy and I shared Communion in the dining hall,
    - She told me how God had blessed her,
      - because someone had given her a new electric wheelchair
    - And she was so excited about the new wheelchair access ramp that our presbyYOUTH group built onto her house a couple weeks ago,
      - and what a wonderful blessing that was ~

Amazingly,
- Through all the struggles Sand has faced and continues to battle,
  - Her faith in Jesus and her love for God and others hasn't wavered ~

Like David,
  - She has answered the Call to Faith with joy and love in her heart,
    - and she depends on the Lord to give her courage and strength each day!

What about you?

How have you responded to The Call to Faith?
- Are you fully trusting God?
  - or are you depending more on the things of this world?

What about our church family?
- Are we living out the Call to Faith?
  - Are we trusting God to provide and guide us forward?
  - Are we living out our faith in action?
  - Are we each doing our part to help our church fulfill our vision?

As we noted last week,

Discovering your life purpose begins with the Call to Follow Jesus ~

- like Peter, we are called to leave our old ways behind,
- and follow Jesus into the future God has planned for us ~

And then, beyond the Call to Follow,
- The next facet of God's Call is
6. <u>The Call to Faith</u> ~
    - Which is really about fully trusting in God,
        - and depending on the Lord,
            ◦ no matter your circumstances,
                - or the struggles you face...

Like David,
- <u>We live in a stressed-out world</u> ~
    - where the pressure to perform and succeed is tremendous...

    - Like our Nebraska Huskers, we may start the season 0-and-5,
        ◦ and be up by 10 points with 5 minutes to go,
        ◦ only to lose another heartbreaker -- on the road -- in overtime...

    - But even then,
        ◦ In our times of deepest stress and loss,
        ◦ **God is still faithful ~**
            - **He will never let you down...**

And – no matter what our circumstances may be,
- <u>God greatly desires our trust and worship</u>

    - Even in moments of stress -- and loss -- and grief -- and terror,
        ◦ God desires that we fully trust Him,
            - and worship Him with all our hearts!

- David-the-Shepherd-Boy trusted God to help him defeat Goliath ~
    - David-the-King trusted God to protect him against his enemies ~

My Life Purpose

- o and throughout his life,
  - David the worshipper expressed his trust in the Lord,
  - by regularly praising God!
- o Whether singing, or dancing,
  - or playing the harp,
- o He made a joyful noise to the Lord ~
  - and offered his heart -- and his life -- to God in worship!

So, let's do the same when we worship ~

- Let your worship be an expression of your love and trust in God!
  - Don't just go through the motions, and sing the lyrics like they don't matter…
  - Let your voice give praise and honor to the Lord,
    - o Lift up the name of Jesus – and express your faith in worship!
      - Draw near to the heart of God,
      - As you respond to the Call to Faith and Trust in Him

  - Give God 100% ~
    - o Go "all in" – and praise the Lord,
      - for He has shown us the wonders of his unfailing love!

You see,

- <u>Depending on God requires complete commitment</u>
  - It's not about giving God just *a portion* of our hearts –
    - o it's trusting God, in and with, **everything** ~

In verse 14,

- When David proclaimed his complete trust in God, even in the face of danger,
- The Hebrew phrase he uses is "*Wa-ani ba-tah-ti a-le-ka Yahweh*"
  - o which is literally translated, "But as for me, **I trust you**, O Yahweh"

- In other words,
  - o David is expressing his faith in -- and reliance upon – Yahweh, the Lord

- He's not depending on his own resourcefulness or effort,
- He's not relying on his army, or his intelligence,
  - or his reputation…
  - He's proclaiming his **complete and utter dependence and trust in God**

That's what it looks like when we respond to God's Call to Faith ~
- It fills our hearts with **peace** and **hope** and **confidence**,
  - not because we are somehow better people once we believe,
  - but because we are **trusting in GOD**, who is forever faithful ~

And then, over time,
- <u>As we live by faith, our love for God grows</u> all the more ~
  - As we learn to **trust** in God through good times and bad,
    - then God's **trustworthy love** grows in us…

  - As we **depend** on God through wins and losses,
    - then God's **dependable love** grows in us…

  - As we **rely** on God through ups and downs,
    - then God's **reliable love** grows in us…

  - For our God is forever faithful ~
    - He will never fail us,
      - or abandon us ~
    - So, open your heart today,
      - to the overwhelming, never-ending love of God!

- <u>**Live by faith – and receive strength and courage** from God</u> ~
  - As David said in verse 24,

  "Be strong and courageous, all you who put your hope in the Lord"!

After all,
- That's how David was able to stand up to Goliath,

My Life Purpose

- o and ultimately defeat him...

- That's how Jonathan was able to protect David,
  - o from the attacks of his father, Saul...

- That's how Peter was able to lead the Church in Jerusalem...

- And that's how you can overcome whatever struggles you are facing ~

<u>Be strong and courageous -- as you trust in God!</u>

For the One who is faithful and trustworthy,
- o The One who stood up to Satan ~
  - defeated sin on the cross,
  - and won victory over death,
  - stands with you!

Jesus loves you – that much!
- He has a wonderful purpose and plan for your life!

So be brave. Be strong. And don't give up.
- Keep the faith. And trust in God.
- Today, tomorrow, and forever.

Amen – Let it be so...

Let's pray...

Heavenly Father, we love you, and we praise you, Lord. Give us faith to live with the strength and courage of David, and to reflect the hope and love of Jesus in the world. This is our purpose – may we live by faith, trusting You, now and always. We pray this in Jesus' name, Amen.

My Life Purpose

REFLECT and RESPOND (Questions for personal or group reflection):

- Read today's Bible passage. How is the Holy Spirit speaking to you?

- From what you know of David's life, what stressors and failures did he face?

- How did David's faith in God help him deal with stress?

- What message of hope does this passage offer?

- Are you fully trusting God in your life?

- How can you encourage others to trust and love God?

The Call to Fellowship

Part 4 of *My Life Purpose: How to Discover God's Call*

Acts 2:42-47

Focus Statement: The Call to Fellowship is an invitation to Christ-centered koinonia.

Function Statement: Pursue God's Call to fellowship and discover your life purpose!

Scripture Reading   Acts 2:42-47 (NIV)

⁴² They devoted themselves to the apostles' teaching and to fellowship, to the breaking of bread and to prayer. ⁴³ Everyone was filled with awe at the many wonders and signs performed by the apostles. ⁴⁴ All the believers were together and had everything in common. ⁴⁵ They sold property and possessions to give to anyone who had need. ⁴⁶ Every day they continued to meet together in the temple courts. They broke bread in their homes and ate together with glad and sincere hearts, ⁴⁷ praising God and enjoying the favor of all the people. And the Lord added to their number daily those who were being saved.

MESSAGE

Let's pray…
Dear Lord, we do thank you and praise you for your Word, and for the way that you continue to work in and through the church, and in our lives. We pray that you will help us to grasp the truth found in this scripture today. Lord, give me your words to speak, for what I say means nothing apart from you. Open our ears, our minds, and our hearts to the message of good news that you have for us this morning. In Jesus name, Amen.

There's a story about a man who was walking through the Sahara Desert,
- desperate for water,
- when he saw something, far off in the distance.

Hoping to find water,
- he walked toward the image,
  - only to find a little old woman sitting at a card table
    - with a bunch of neckties laid out on it.

The thirsty man asked, "Please, I'm dying of thirst, can I have some water?"

The woman replied, "I don't have any water, but why don't you buy a tie?"
"Here's one that goes nicely with your outfit."

The man shouted, "I don't want a tie, lady -- I need water!"

"Okay, don't buy a tie. But to show you what a nice person I am,
I'll tell you that over that hill there, about four miles, is a nice restaurant.
Walk that way, they'll give you all the water you want."

The dehydrated soul thanked the woman
- and walked away toward the hill and eventually disappeared...

Three hours later...
- he returned, crawling back to where the woman was still sitting behind her card table.

She said "I told you, about four miles over that hill. Couldn't you find it?"

The man rasped, "I found it all right. They wouldn't let me in without a tie."

You know, a lot of times our sense of community is kind of like this story.
- We gather together, thirsty for meaning and purpose in life...
    - Thirsty for relationships...
    - Thirsty for joy, and happiness...
- But it's like we never stop thinking about our own thirst ~
    - It's like we just come together looking for what's-in-it-for-me...
    - The result is that we don't really connect in true community ~
    - We gather together in the same place –
        - or these days, on the same social media,
        - and we're looking for connection,
    - But we remain alone, on our own individual journey,
        - because we are fundamentally selfish...

- o And the result, is that some of us nearly die of thirst in the process…

More often than not,

- our sense of community is more like **lumped loneliness** than **true togetherness**
  - o We are more like a group of lonely people lumped in the same place,
    - continually disappointed and thirsty for something more…
  - o Than a "called community" marked by true togetherness

- So, maybe we need some help
  - o Maybe we need to learn some new ways of allowing the Holy Spirit to work in us,
    - to build authentic Christ-centered community among us…
  - o And so today we will be looking back at the early church…

We will look and see how the Acts 2 church experienced true togetherness…

7. And then ask ourselves -- how The Call to Fellowship can help us today…

Of course, as we see in verse 42,

- The Call to Fellowship starts with **devoted hearts** (v. 42)
  - The Greek word used here for "devoted" is *proskartereō*
    - o And it literally means "to persist or persevere" –
      - "to keep on – with devotion"
      - This means they weren't just "going through the motions"
      - their hearts were in it --
      - they were fully invested
    - o They DEVOTED themselves to living out the Call to Fellowship
      - they sought genuine connection and authentic community,
      - and they worked hard to build it and strengthen it…

But the real draw for their devotion -- was *Jesus* ~

- Because the Call to Fellowship is an invitation to **Christ-centered *koinonia*** –
  - meaning it's a call to *experience Christ* in relationships with one another ~
    - o In fact, *koinonia* -- the Greek word for fellowship –
      - suggests a close mutual association,

- sharing a common bond or "communion" in Christ –
- And so *koinonia* is not just about being in a group of like-minded people,
    - occupying the same space ~

- It's about sharing the deep bond of Christ-centered community ~
    - It's about enjoying the presence and love of Jesus together ~

- You see, there is no true *koinonia* without Christ's Spirit in us -- and between us ~
    - *Jesus* is what we have in common ~
    - He draws us into oneness,
        - and loves each of us through each other
    - Such Christ-centered fellowship is what we are created for ~
        - it's part of our life purpose – and God's design for us ~

- And so, the early church was intentional about making time just to be together –
    - to experience Christ in fellowship with one another

In this way, the Call to Fellowship
- is really about **togetherness** ~
    - Verse 44 says that
    "All the believers WERE TOGETHER, and *had everything in common*"
        - And so, not only were they together "in the same place"
            - but by the power of the Holy Spirit,
            - they were the ultimate example of "true togetherness" and unity ~
        - They shared Christ together ~
            - They shared faith -- and hope -- and love together...
        - And of course,
            - They shared meals together ~
    - Verse 46 says
    "Every day they continued to meet together in the temple courts."
    "They broke bread in their homes and ate together with glad and sincere hearts"

Even though Jesus was no longer with them physically,
- when they broke bread together,
- it was like they felt his presence with them,
- and their sense of togetherness was strengthened…

Maybe eating together reminded them of sharing meals with Jesus…
- or perhaps, there is something special that happens when we eat together ~

Somehow, our sense of togetherness grows when we sit around the table,
- and share our lives with one another,
- enjoying good conversation,
- laughter,
- and good food together…

There is something about eating together that builds true togetherness ~

But breaking bread wasn't all the early church did to share in the common life together
- verse 45 says,

    "They sold property and possessions **to give** to anyone who had need."

You see, the Call to Fellowship also
- <u>inspires **sharing**</u> what we have with others ~

    - For sharing and generosity is a natural result of true togetherness ~
        - In that first church,
        - the newly born believers were together,
        - and they shared their possessions ~

    - They had been liberated to live for Christ and each other ~
        - And in giving of their time and material possessions,
        - they found that God grew their bonds of togetherness even stronger…

    - There was none of the defensive clutching-of-their-own-wealth
        - which is so evident in our culture today ~

    - For sharing and helping others is an important quality of Christian fellowship ~

My Life Purpose

And in many ways,
- It's one thing that truly sets us apart ~

When our youth and adult Mission Team went to Puerto Rico this summer,
- We came across a number of people in desperate need ~
    - They were lonely...
    - They felt forgotten...
    - And many of them had very little as far as material possessions...
- And so, when we heard their stories and saw their needs,
    - whether it was to repair their roof, or replace a window...
    - or whether it was to simply show we cared (and that God cared) ...
- When we saw their needs,
    - our church family stepped up and shared all we could with them ~
        - sometimes this meant paying for construction materials out of our own pockets
        - other times it meant stopping the work, and listening, and praying with them

But some of the most powerful moments came,
- when the Puerto Rican people did the same for us ~
    - They were inspired to prepare meals for us,
    - They opened their homes to a bunch of strangers from Nebraska...
        - And it was awesome ~
        - We enjoyed genuine Christian fellowship (and authentic Puerto Rican food) together...
        - Even though we spoke different languages,
            - we shared a common bond...
    - And when we prayed together, often in English and Spanish,
        - It was like the doors of heaven opened and God's love rained down on us!

And then, as we went about our work,
- and the bonds of Christian fellowship grew stronger throughout the week,
    - there were more and more smiles – and laughter – and joy ~
        - both within our group – and in the faces of our Puerto Rican friends...

Because the Call to Fellowship
- <u>generates praise and goodwill</u> –
    - not only within the church, but also in the world!

Verse 47 says that the Christians in Acts 2 were

"praising God -- and enjoying the favor of *all the people*."

You see,
- When the church is being the Church ~
- When we live in genuine Christian community,
    - and we help others in need ~
- When we enjoy being together,
    - and we offer praise to God ~
- When we show our love for God and one another,
    - through prayer,
    - through praise,
    - or through our actions ~
        - then hearts are lifted up!

For when we connect, grow and serve together,
- And the world sees us giving thanks to God in all circumstances,
- and enjoying one another with glad and sincere hearts,
- then the world takes notice!

Praising God with the way we live has that impact on people ~
- For which person will receive more goodwill from others:
    1) the person who constantly *whines* and *complains* about life,
        - and is filled with *negativity?*
    2) or the person who gives credit to God for blessings,
        - looks for ways to bless others,
        - and praises God even in the midst of difficult times?

Even more – which will it be for you?
- Will you devote yourself to living out God's purposes in Christian community?
  - OR -
- Will you devote yourself to pursuing your own selfish purposes?

After all, ~ over the course of time, your life will reflect what you are devoted to ~
- And the same is true for our life as a church family ~
  - We will reflect what we are devoted to ~

So, let's carefully consider the Call to Fellowship,
- And let's devote ourselves to fulfilling it in our life together ~

Essentially, let's Be The Church as God originally designed it to be ~

Let's live out the <u>Four Practices of a Vital Church</u> as revealed in Acts 2 ~

May our life together be marked by a
- <u>Devotion to Teaching God's Word</u> ~

  - For from its beginning, the early church devoted itself to biblical teaching ~
    - They spent time listening to the apostles teach about Jesus...
    - They spent time reciting and singing the Psalms...
    - And the power of the Word proclaimed by people like Peter and Paul
      - brought many people to faith,
      - and continues to do so today...

  - Let's be that kind of church!
    - Let's be devoted to teaching God's Word!
    - Let's be devoted to applying the Bible to our lives!
    - Let's be devoted to living out God's Purposes in the world!

And as we do,

    May our life together also be marked by a

- <u>Devotion to Fellowship</u> ~
    - Just as the early church broke bread together,
        - and enjoyed sharing meals together in their homes,
    - Let's be intentional about connecting in fellowship together ~
        - Whether it's making the effort to introduce yourself to someone new,
        - inviting another church member or family over for a meal,
        - or connecting in one of our many fellowship groups ~
    - Find a way to grow in Christian community with others –

    - Devote yourself to building the bonds of koinonia fellowship,
        - And God will bless and grow our church family!

Of course, let's also continue our strong

- <u>Devotion to Sharing</u> ~
    - Let's continue to be a church family that helps those in need ~
        - And there are so many ways we do this, as a church ~

        - We don't just host the Summer Lunch Program,
            - we make sure any child who needs a backpack and school supplies gets one…
        - We don't just talk about the call to missions,
            - We give financial and prayer support to our mission partners,
            - and we send youth and adults on mission trips…
        - We don't just make and sell 3000 apple and cherry pies
            - to support missions and outreach,
            - we share about our lives and make new friends,
            - as we have fun making dough balls, peeling apples,
            - rolling out pie crusts, and crimping edges…

So, let's keep growing in our devotion to sharing ~

- and when God puts someone in our midst who has need,
    - or when our hearts are moved to give,
    - let's be generous in sharing our gifts and resources,
    - as well as sharing our love and friendship!

But, perhaps above all,

May our life together also be marked by a

- Devotion to Prayer ~
    - For the early church was fully devoted to prayer…
        - They knew the power of prayer firsthand,
        - and were led in their life together by prayer…
    - They shared common prayers that were passed on from generation to generation…
    - They prayed the psalms, and they prayed the Lord's Prayer…
    - They prayed alone, and they prayed together…
    - They spoke to God, and they listened for God…
    - They were devoted to prayer ~

- For they knew –
    - that when people pray together,
    - they stay together ~
    - and it's through the power of prayer that lives are changed ~

So, let's be devoted to Prayer ~

- Let's seek God with all our hearts,
    - And when we're not sure how to pray,
    - Let's remember that the Holy Spirit intercedes for us,
        - and interprets our groans and jumbled prayers to the Father
        - Who hears and knows our hearts…
    - So, if prayer is a challenge for you, ask the Holy Spirit for help ~
        - For when you are open to the Spirit in your heart,
        - you are already experiencing the power of prayer…

Let's be a church of Prayer ~

- Let's pray for one another,
- Let's pray for our ministries,
- Let's pray for our community,
- Let's pray for our country,
- Let's pray for all countries and all people –

For there is perhaps no greater privilege we enjoy as Christians than to pray together ~

- For when God's people pray together,
  - the Lord listens
    - and lives are changed…

In Acts 2, the church devoted themselves

- to the apostles' teaching,
- and to fellowship,
- to the breaking of bread,
- and to prayer ~

And as verse 47 says,

"the Lord added to their number daily, those who were being saved."

May it be so with us ~

- May we be devoted to Teaching God's Word,
- To Fellowship,
- To Sharing,
- And to Prayer

May we <u>Pursue God's Call to fellowship</u>

- <u>and discover our life purpose</u> together!

Let's pray…
Heavenly Father, you have called us into this fellowship, and you have a wonderful vision and purpose for our life together. We pray that our hearts would be fully devoted to Jesus – guided by your Word and empowered by the Holy Spirit to change lives. We love you, Lord, and it's in the mighty and beautiful name of Jesus we pray, Amen.

REFLECT and RESPOND (Questions for personal or group reflection):

- Read today's Bible passage. How is the Holy Spirit speaking to you?

- What does it mean to be devoted to something or someone?

- Who or what are you devoted to?

- Why is spiritual fellowship vital to healthy Christians and churches?

- How has Christian fellowship impacted your life?

The Call to a Special Function

Part 5 of *My Life Purpose: How to Discover God's Call*

Romans 12:3-8

> Focus Statement: God's call is for you to use your gifts for the good of others.
>
> Function Statement: Use your gifts and discover God's call for your life!

Scripture Reading   Romans 12:3-8 (NLT)

³ Because of the privilege and authority God has given me, I give each of you this warning: Don't think you are better than you really are. Be honest in your evaluation of yourselves, measuring yourselves by the faith God has given us. ⁴ Just as our bodies have many parts and each part has a special function, ⁵ so it is with Christ's body. We are many parts of one body, and we all belong to each other.

⁶ In his grace, God has given us different gifts for doing certain things well. So, if God has given you the ability to prophesy, speak out with as much faith as God has given you. ⁷ If your gift is serving others, serve them well. If you are a teacher, teach well. ⁸ If your gift is to encourage others, be encouraging. If it is giving, give generously. If God has given you leadership ability, take the responsibility seriously. And if you have a gift for showing kindness to others, do it gladly.

MESSAGE

Let's pray...
Heavenly Father, you created each of us with special gifts, and called us together as the body of Christ. Open our hearts and minds today and speak into our souls with your Word. Transform us, O Lord, in the power of Jesus' name, Amen.

Sally was driving home from one of her business trips in northern Arizona

- when she saw an elderly Navajo woman walking on the side of the road.

As the trip was a long and quiet one,

- she stopped the car and asked the woman if she would like a ride.

With a silent nod of thanks, the woman got into the car.

Resuming the journey, Sally tried in vain to make a bit of small talk with the Navajo woman.
- The old woman just sat silently, looking at everything she saw,
- studying every little detail, until she noticed a white bag on the seat next to Sally.

"What's in the bag?" asked the old woman.

Sally looked down at the bag and, smiling, said,
  "It's a box of chocolates. I got it for my husband."

The Navajo woman was silent for another moment or two…

Then, speaking with the quiet wisdom of an elder, she said: "Good trade."

Do you ever wonder,
- What is the true value of my life?
- Am I worth more than a box of chocolates?!
- What is my purpose?
- Why am I here?

We've been talking in this series about How to Discover God's Call - or Purpose - for your life
- So far, we've explored three of the Five Facets of God's Call:
    - We've talked about the **Call to Follow** –
        - (for discovering God's purpose begins with turning from our old ways,
            - and choosing to follow Jesus…)
    - A couple Sundays ago, we've focused on the **Call to Faith** –
        - (for living into God's purpose means trusting God with your life…)
    - And last week, we explored the **Call to Fellowship** –
        - and we discovered that -- as the body of Christ –
        - we are called to be in authentic Christian community together…

The fourth facet of God's Call builds on the others ~
- For within the body of Christ,

  We are each <u>Called to a Special Function</u> ~
    - We are each given gifts from God -

- that are given for a purpose –
    - to be used – for the good of the body ~

Still, in Romans 12, verse 3, Paul begins with a stern warning:

- He says to <u>Be careful not to think too highly of yourself</u> (v. 3)
    - "Don't think you are better than you really are," he writes ~
    - "Be honest in your evaluation of yourselves."

Because Paul knows that for most of us,

- Our problem when it comes to thinking about our self-worth
    - tends to be a problem with PRIDE, not with HUMILITY…
- We tend to over-value our significance ~
    - We tend to base our sense of self-worth on our accomplishments ~
        - or the value of our possessions…

But Paul urges us that there is another way ~

- "Don't think too highly of yourselves…"
- <u>Instead, measure yourselves by the faith and gifts God</u> has given you ~
    - In other words, measure your sense of self-worth by your God-given gifts ~
        - and by the faith God has given you in using them,
        - not by the amount of money you have,
        - or even by what you produce in life ~
    - Because what really matters – is not just what you do for God,
        - but what God can do through you – and your gifts ~

    - As the late Eugene Petersen paraphrased Paul's words in *The Message*,
      "The only accurate way to understand ourselves
       is by what God is and by what he does for us,
       not by what we are and what we do for him."

Still, Paul wants you and I to recognize and remember, that

- <u>As part of Christ's body, God gives you a special function</u> –
    - a purposeful role to play –

- o and provides you with the necessary gifts to make your unique contribution ~
- Paul writes,

    "Just as our bodies have many parts and each part has a special function, so it is with Christ's body. We are many parts of one body, and we all belong to each other"

And so, you see, YOU ARE SO SPECIAL ~

- God has chosen you and gifted you for a special function ~
    - a divine purpose...
    - a unique calling...
    - a purposeful activity for which you have been specially gifted...
- And yet at the same time,
    - your value and giftedness come from being a part of Christ's body ~
        - for apart from Christ, you can do nothing...
        - As John wrote in his gospel (and we'll talk about this more next week)
        - a branch that is separated from the vine, withers and dies...

So yes, you have a special function to fulfill within the body of Christ ~

- and as you may know,
- and our church's statement of purpose is to "passionately pursue the call of Christ"
    - this means each of us is tasked with using our gifts
        - to passionately pursue our God-given, pursue ~
    - Collectively, we have identified that our common purpose
        - is to "Love God. Love People. (and) Change Lives."
    - But the way each one of us pursues that call varies –
        - and is largely shaped by the gifts God has given us –
        - and by the special function God has called each of us to fulfill...

As Paul wrote in verse 6,

"In his grace, God has given us different gifts for doing certain things well."

Unfortunately, far too often, apart from his grace,

- We compare ourselves to others,
    - And we somehow think that our gifts are either better than theirs,

- or we see others use their gifts, and we think we "could never do that" ~

But when we play the "comparison game" with others, we are completely missing the point ~. Because the fact is,

- <u>God has given each of us different gifts **as signs of his grace**</u> ~
  - In other words, God's gracious gift to us ~
    - is to give each of us a special function ~
    - to bless each of us with a unique role to play,
- God didn't just throw us together randomly,
  - or call us together by chance ~

- God has uniquely gifted and called each one of us together with a special purpose ~
  - And the diversity of gifts, experiences, abilities and perspectives that we all bring
    - is an expression of God's abundant grace –
    - For The Lord is not limited in ability!
    - And The Lord is not limited in power!
    - **"In his grace,** God has given us all different gifts"
      - And when we each do our part,
      - When we offer our gifts *in His grace,*
      - and passionately pursue the calling of Christ together,
      - then the power of God's grace is fully activated and unleashed,
      - in and through us!

    - This is the Good News of God's Call for our lives!
      - and it's so exciting to be a part of!

    - There's something so special about seeing the body of Christ at work ~
      - with each one of us offering our gifts,
      - and giving it our all,
      - simply because that is what God has called us to do!

Unfortunately, there are times when some of us hold back...

- We either don't offer or use our gifts,
- Or we only use them for personal gain,
  - rather than offering them to God's purposes…

For example,
- Perhaps God has given you the gift of leadership ~
  - but you're only using that gift to grow your worldly influence -- and affluence,
    - rather than using your gift to strengthen the body of Christ ~
- Or perhaps God has blessed you with the gift of being an encourager,
  - but you only give encouragement to people
    - who you think can offer you something in return…

Sadly,
- far too often, we withhold our gifts,
  - or we only use them when we stand to benefit personally…

Therefore, I join the Apostle Paul in urging you today,
- To <u>Dedicate your gifts to **God's service**,</u>
  - <u>not simply to your own personal gain</u> (v. 6-8)
  - So whatever gifts God has blessed you with,
    - use them in service to God ~
      - and watch what happens,
      - when God works through you – and through us, as the body of Christ –
      - to achieve the Lord's purposes…

I love how Eugene Peterson describes what this looks like in *The Message* ~

He writes,

> **4-6** In this way we are like the various parts of a human body. Each part gets its meaning from the body as a whole, not the other way around. The body we're talking about is Christ's body of chosen people. Each of us finds our meaning and function as a part of his body.
> But as a chopped-off finger or cut-off toe, we wouldn't amount to much, would we?

So, since we find ourselves fashioned into all these excellently formed and marvelously functioning parts in Christ's body, let's just go ahead and be what we were made to be, without enviously or pridefully comparing ourselves with each other, or trying to be something we aren't.

6-8 If you preach, just preach God's Message, nothing else; if you help, just help, don't take over; if you teach, stick to your teaching; if you give encouraging guidance, be careful that you don't get bossy; if you're put in charge, don't manipulate; if you're called to give aid to people in distress, keep your eyes open and be quick to respond; if you work with the disadvantaged, don't let yourself get irritated with them or depressed by them. Keep a smile on your face.

In short, what Paul is saying,
- is to <u>Be generous in using your gifts to fulfill God's special purpose</u> (v. 8)
    - Don't hold back!
    - Jump in and get to it!
    - Be engaged in the life of the Church!
    - Use whatever you're good at -- to advance God's purposes!
    - For God has called you to a special function –
        - and the Lord's desire is that you passionately pursue that call,
            - with everything you've got!

That's what I love so much about the Apple Pie Mission Fundraiser ~
- It's such a beautiful picture of what it looks like to Be The Church ~
- to be the Body of Christ, serving together ~
    - with each one of us doing our part, and using our gifts ~
        - Those who have the gift of administration are keeping things organized...
        - Those who have the gift of hospitality are helping everyone to have fun...
        - Those who have the gift of slicing sticks of margarine, are slicing away...

It doesn't matter how old you are,
- or how experienced you are ~
    - everyone can offer the gift of their time and effort
        - and serve with a smile on your face ~

- It's as simple as signing up for a shift -- or two -- or three,
    - and showing up to help ~
- Whether it's helping to make 6000 doughballs,
    - helping to peel and core 80 cases of apples,
    - helping to assemble 3000 pies…
    - or helping to welcome with a smile,
    - all those who come to pick up their delicious pies!
- Everyone can help ~
    - and every gift of service is vital to us accomplishing our goal ~
- In fact,
    - The ONLY way we can meet our goal is by the whole body working together,
        - using our gifts to make a difference…
    - So, I hope you'll come be a part of the fun this week ~
        - Use your gifts for good –
            - and help strengthen our church family as you do!

After all, that's really what this is all about ~

That's the <u>Life Application</u> for us today ~

- For although <u>We are all different, we belong to one another</u>
    - God has given us different gifts and abilities…
        - yet every gift is needed and valuable…
    - It's kind of like with the Husker football team ~
        - It took a while to figure out the gifts of each member of the team,
        - But in time, they realized they belong to one another –
            - and every member has something to offer – for the good of the team
        - Whether it's strength and speed,
            - skill and athleticism,
            - or pure heart and effort…
        - When each part offers all they've got,
            - then good things happen ~

For example, last week against Minnesota,
- ○ When Eric Lee hustled all the way down the field to make a touchdown-saving tackle on a kick return, he gave it everything he had ~
- ○ and a few plays later,
  - - another Husker defender got an interception,
  - - and the tide turned for good...

It took the unique contributions from each player for the team to find its first victory ~

And it's similar with the body of Christ ~
- <u>By design, not one person has all the gifts</u>
  - - It's a team effort ~
    - ○ God gives each of us a unique mix of gifts, interests, and abilities,
      - - And none of us have ALL the gifts ~
      - - We need each other ~
    - ○ We need people who pray continually...
    - ○ We need people who encourage endlessly...
    - ○ We need people who teach passionately...
    - ○ We need people who can lead and organize efficiently...
    - ○ We need people who are eager to serve faithfully...
    - ○ We need people who give generously...
    - ○ We need people who love wholeheartedly...
    - ○ We need people who care selflessly...
    - ○ We need every person to use the gifts God has given them...

For the reality is
- <u>The body of Christ is healthiest when each part fulfills its function</u>

And this has been God's design all along,
- to give each of us a unique mix of gifts,
  - ○ so that when all of us use our gifts,
    - ▪ the body of Christ changes lives ~

My Life Purpose

- o For as the Lord works through us together,
  - God takes what we offer,
    - and multiplies our gifts to meet needs ~
    - (much like what Jesus did with the loaves and the fishes, to feed thousands of hungry people)

For when we each give from the heart,
- using our God-given gifts for the good of the body,
  - o there is a sort of exponential - spiritual - synergy that results ~
    - and the outcome of what we can do together,
      - is greater than the combined sum of our individual efforts...

And while this is true – and part of God's beautiful design for the church,
- There's also a flip side... ~

And here it is ~
- <u>If you're not using your gifts, the rest of the body suffers</u>
  - In 1 Corinthians 12,
    - o Paul describes how the variety of gifts within the body of Christ are inter-connected, and vital to one another ~

      He writes,

      "This makes for harmony among the members, so that all the members care for each other. If one part suffers, all the parts suffer with it, and if one part is honored, all the parts are glad.

      All of you together are Christ's body, and each of you is a part of it." (v. 25-27)

So... how would you say you're doing?

- What special function has God gifted you for?

- How are you using the gifts God has given you?

- Are you giving your best to God and others?

Brothers and sisters in Christ,

- <u>God's call -- is for you to use your gifts -- for the good of others</u>
    - This is central to your life purpose ~
        - God has called you to a special function ~
            - and the Lord's purpose and plan for your life,
            - is that you would use your gifts to bless others ~

So that's the challenge – and the promise -- we are left with today ~

It's not complicated.

Simply put:

<u>Use your God-given gifts -- and discover God's call for your life!</u>

And you know what?

- I'm excited and honored to be on the journey with you.

Let's pray…

Heavenly Father, we love you – and we thank you for blessing each of us with a special function – and with the gifts needed to pursue it. Lead us forward, O Lord, and work through us to change lives. We pray all this in Jesus' name, Amen.

REFLECT and RESPOND (Questions for personal or group reflection):

- Read today's Bible passage. How is the Holy Spirit speaking to you?

- How do people today typically measure their self-worth?

- What warning does Paul offer in verse 3?

- What solution does Paul suggest – and how does this impact what you think of yourself?

- What special function has God gifted you for?

- How are you using the gifts God has given?

The Call to Be Fruitful

Part 6 of *My Life Purpose: How to Discover God's Call*

John 15:1-17

> Focus Statement: The Call to be Fruitful is centered on Christ's command: love each other.
>
> Function Statement: Continue in Christ's love and discover God's call to a fruitful life!

Scripture Reading   John 15:1-17 (NLT)

¹ "I am the true grapevine, and my Father is the gardener. ² He cuts off every branch of mine that doesn't produce fruit, and he prunes the branches that do bear fruit so they will produce even more. ³ You have already been pruned and purified by the message I have given you. ⁴ Remain in me, and I will remain in you. For a branch cannot produce fruit if it is severed from the vine, and you cannot be fruitful unless you remain in me. ⁵ "Yes, I am the vine; you are the branches. Those who remain in me, and I in them, will produce much fruit. For apart from me you can do nothing. ⁶ Anyone who does not remain in me is thrown away like a useless branch and withers. Such branches are gathered into a pile to be burned. ⁷ But if you remain in me and my words remain in you, you may ask for anything you want, and it will be granted! ⁸ When you produce much fruit, you are my true disciples. This brings great glory to my Father. ⁹ "I have loved you even as the Father has loved me. Remain in my love. ¹⁰ When you obey my commandments, you remain in my love, just as I obey my Father's commandments and remain in his love. ¹¹ I have told you these things so that you will be filled with my joy. Yes, your joy will overflow! ¹² This is my commandment: Love each other in the same way I have loved you. ¹³ There is no greater love than to lay down one's life for one's friends. ¹⁴ You are my friends if you do what I command. ¹⁵ I no longer call you slaves, because a master doesn't confide in his slaves. Now you are my friends, since I have told you everything the Father told me. ¹⁶ You didn't choose me. I chose you. I appointed you to go and produce lasting fruit, so that the Father will give you whatever you ask for, using my name. ¹⁷ This is my command: Love each other.

MESSAGE

Let's pray...

Father in Heaven,

We thank you for your Word and for the gift of life with You and with each other. Lord, give me your words to speak, for the things I say mean nothing apart from you. Holy Spirit, open our ears and our hearts so that we might hear Your truth and be transformed according to Your will. In Jesus' name, Amen.

My Life Purpose

A week ago, I got a random text message from an old friend – Jeremiah Lange
- Some of you have met Jeremiah before –
    - he gave the message at my installation service here 7 years ago...
- And 5 years before that,
    - I gave the message at his ordination service as he prepared to serve as Pastor of First Presbyterian Church of Marion, Kansas...

- But our history goes way back to 1995,
    - When Jen and I first started as the Youth Director at St. Andrew's Presbyterian Church in Tucson, AZ, and Jeremiah was a high school student in our youth group
    - But he was also a leader with our Jr. High Ministry,
    - He played the "slinky" in our youth worship band,
    - and his big heart for Jesus made church fun and life-changing for many people

- So, when he messaged me last Monday and said he was on his way up to Fremont with a member of his Kansas Church to watch the member's son play in the Midland University Warriors vs. Nebraska Wesleyan Prairie Wolves junior varsity football game,
    - Jen and I re-arranged our plans, so we could see Jeremiah ~
        - even though it was only for a short visit,
        - sitting together in the stands at Heedum Field,
        - enjoying the bonds of friendship that began some 23 years ago...

Do you have friendships like that?
- Friendships where you cannot see the person for months – or even years at a t time –
    - And then when you re-connect it's like you never missed a beat?!
    - You instantly pick up where you left off – and you just understand each other ~
        - It's like your connection goes beyond just shared history and experience ~
            - and there's a unity of Christian friendship,
                - that is lifelong and enduring?

My Life Purpose

I believe God designed us for those kinds of relationships
- I believe that's part of our life purpose ~
    - to connect, grow, and serve together in genuine Christian community ~
    - to live as brothers and sisters in Christ who love God, love people and change lives
- And I believe that it's through these relational connections that our lives bear fruit ~
    - and that we are called to be fruitful…

I believe this, because that's what Jesus believed ~
- It's what he taught ~
- and it's how he lived ~

So, this morning,
- I'd like to reflect for a few moments on the words of Jesus to his disciples in John 15,
    - as he was preparing them to go into the world and make disciples

To help them understand his message,
- Jesus chose to use an illustration of
1. <u>The True Vine and the Branches</u>,
    - to describe the nature of his relationship with them ~

- For Jesus wanted them to see that
    - <u>He is the Vine,</u>
    - <u>The Father is the Gardener,</u>
    - <u>and We are the Branches…</u>

But to help us really grasp what Jesus means by this,
- Let me share a little background for context ~

You see, as Jesus was teaching all this to his disciples,
- they were together in Jerusalem,
- on their way from the Upper Room where they had recently shared the Last Supper,
    - → and heading to the Garden of Gethsemane,
        - where Jesus would pray, and eventually be arrested…

Along the way, they would have passed the Temple ~
- Now, Jesus knew that one of the chief ornaments on the Temple
    - was a huge golden vine with a cluster of grapes as large as Peter ~
- And so, you can imagine Jesus pointing to the huge bunch of fruit and saying,
    - "See that grapevine up there?"
    - "I am the true vine, and my Father is the gardener."

And then Jesus added that God the Gardener
> 1) **removes** unfruitful, dead branches…
> 2) and **prunes** healthy branches so they can bear more fruit…

And I don't know about you, but my guess is the disciples' minds were running wild now ~
- Which of them had been "unfruitful" and in danger of being cut off?
    - Was it Judas, the Betrayer?
- Which of them needed "pruning"?
    - Was it Peter, who Jesus predicted would deny Him three times?
    - Was it Thomas, who had a tendency to doubt everything?

With all these questions likely swirling in their heads,
> Jesus said again in verse 5,
>   - "Yes, I am the vine; you are the branches."
>   - "Those who remain in me, and I in them, will produce much fruit."

You see, even with all the uncertainty and self-doubt,
- Jesus reminded his disciples that they **ARE connected** to Him,
    - and that they simply needed to *remain* connected to Him ~
- And the same is true for you and I ~
    - We must remain connected to Jesus to produce fruit
        - For apart from Christ,
            - we can do nothing of lasting value…

My Life Purpose

I imagine, as the disciples listened to Jesus,
- they likely recalled his words from earlier in the day,
    - when he said,
        - "I am the way, and the truth, and the life.
        - No one comes to the Father except through me."

And so now,
- As Jesus explains to his disciples that in order to bear fruit,
    - they must stay connected to Jesus, the Vine – the "way, the truth and the life" –
    - perhaps the message is starting to sink in...

    "Jesus is our source of life."
    "With Jesus, anything is possible – and our lives are purposeful and fruitful!"
    "But apart from Jesus, we are like useless branches that wither and die..."
    "We need to stay connected to Jesus, the Vine – and thankfully,"
    "He has promised to remain connected to us!"

In fact,
- If we look more closely,
    - we see that Jesus uses the verb,
        - "to remain" or "to abide" TEN TIMES in this passage ~
    - And when he says, "Remain in me,"
        - which also means "dwell in me" or "stay in me",
        - he uses the command form of the verb ~

- Eugene Peterson's, *The Message*, translates the command this way,

    "Live in me. Make your home in me just as I do in you." (Isn't that awesome?!)

    But there's more – because then Jesus makes the connection
    - to abiding (or remaining) in God's love, by adding:

    "I've loved you the way my Father has loved me. Make yourselves at home in my love. If you keep my commands, you'll remain intimately at home in my love."

You see,
- o Jesus has moved in to the hearts of his believers –
    - and he invites us to make our home in Him as well…
- o The idea is that we are to take up residence in Jesus,
    - for it is in Him that we find our true home,
    - and our true calling and purpose…

Wow.

What a promise.

What a gift.

Jesus invites us to *make ourselves at home in his love* ~
- In fact, <u>He commands us to love each other,</u>
    - <u>and remain in His love</u>

As he said in verse 11 and 12,
"I have told you these things so that you will be filled with my joy."
"Yes, your joy will overflow!"
"This is my commandment: **Love each other in the same way I have loved you.**"

Of course,
- For us, loving each other is already hard enough –
    - o let alone loving each other *in the same way* Jesus has loved us ~

For Jesus goes on to say that
"There is no greater love than to lay down one's life for one's friends" ~

And that's exactly what Jesus did for us ~
- He laid down his life for us ~ his friends
    - o He remained committed to loving us,
        - all the way to the cross…

And so, we learn from his example,
- That <u>the greatest love among friends is</u> **sacrificial** (v. 13-15)
    - It's being willing to serve the needs of your friends...
    - It's putting them first, before yourself...
    - It's giving sacrificially – of your time, effort and resources...

In 1 Corinthians 13, the Apostle Paul describes such sacrificial agape love as follows:
- (again, from *The Message*):

If I speak with human eloquence and angelic ecstasy but don't love, I'm nothing but the creaking of a rusty gate.
2 If I speak God's Word with power, revealing all his mysteries and making everything plain as day, and if I have faith that says to a mountain, "Jump," and it jumps, but I don't love, I'm nothing.
3-7 If I give everything I own to the poor and even go to the stake to be burned as a martyr, but I don't love, I've gotten nowhere. So, no matter what I say, what I believe, and what I do, I'm bankrupt without love.

Love never gives up.
Love cares more for others than for self.
Love doesn't want what it doesn't have.
Love doesn't strut,
Doesn't have a swelled head,
Doesn't force itself on others,
Isn't always "me first,"
Doesn't fly off the handle,
Doesn't keep score of the sins of others,
Doesn't revel when others grovel,
Takes pleasure in the flowering of truth,
Puts up with anything,

My Life Purpose

Trusts God always,

Always looks for the best,

Never looks back,

But keeps going to the end.

8-10 Love never dies.

(pause)

And so, Church, the call to Love like Jesus is closely linked to

2. The Call to Be Fruitful…
   - It doesn't begin with you or me ~
   - It's not about us, really ~
   - It <u>begins with Jesus choosing to love you</u> ~
   - You see, Jesus told his disciples in v. 16,

     "You did not choose me. I chose you."

     "I appointed you to go and produce lasting fruit."
   - And this is significant ~
     - Because the normal practice of the Jewish culture
       - was that disciples would choose their teacher –

       (they would choose who they wanted to learn from and be mentored by)
   - But with Jesus, it's the other way around ~
     - *Jesus* chose his followers…

Jesus pursued and specifically chose each one of his disciples,

   - and sent them on a mission – to go and bear fruit ~

And in the same way,
   - The Call to be Fruitful for each of us,
     - <u>is about **Jesus** appointing **YOU** to produce lasting fruit</u> –

My Life Purpose

For the Lord has pursued and specifically chosen YOU –
- and has appointed YOU to fulfill a special function,
- and a specific purpose -- that produces lasting spiritual fruit ~ that's your life purpose –

But let's be clear here ~
- "Fruitfulness" is not the same as "productivity" –
- Jesus didn't appoint you to be his slave,
    - in order to accomplish a certain task, or produce something for him...
- In fact,
    - Jesus specifically said we are "NOT his slaves", but his "friends" ~
    - and not just any old friends, but friends that he was willing to die for...

And so, the Call to Be Fruitful
- It is not about WHAT YOU DO,
    - it is about WHO YOU KNOW...

You see, fruitfulness is the result of the Son's life being reproduced in a disciple ~
- The disciple's part is to remain connected to the vine...
- And before long,
    - the character of Christ begins to grow in the life of the disciple ~
    - A little fruit called **love** begins to show up on the branch
    - And then **joy** blossoms
    - And **peace** begins to find its place

As the character of Christ grows in the heart of a disciple who is remaining connected to the vine,
- the branch develops tremendous **patience**,
- Incredible **kindness**,
- Christlike **goodness**,
- Obedient **faithfulness**,
- Godly **gentleness**,
- and the type of **self-control** that reflects the heart of Christ

The Apostle Paul spoke of such fruit of the Spirit in Galatians 5 ~
- where we see that the Call to be Fruitful
  - <u>produces spiritual fruit like love, joy, peace, patience, kindness, goodness, faithfulness, gentleness and self-control –</u>

Sounds pretty good doesn't it?!?
- If you could choose to fill your life with these things, wouldn't you do it in a heartbeat?
- Unfortunately, we don't just *choose* to be fruitful
- We don't just wake up one day and say,
  - "I'm going to choose to be fruitful and fill my life with love, joy, peace, patience, kindness, goodness, faithfulness, gentleness, and self-control..."
- But we can choose to **follow Jesus** as his disciple ~
  - We can choose to **remain** in him...
  - We can choose to **love** others...

And when we make these choices,
- by God's grace, the fruit of the Spirit *will* grow in our lives...

And as Jesus noted in verse 16,
- the result of this spiritual alignment with the Lord,
  - <u>is God giving you whatever you ask for -- in Christ's name</u>
  - because if your heart is filled with the fruit of the Spirit,
  - and if you remain connected to the Vine,
  - then whatever you ask for in Christ's name,
    - would be in alignment with the heart of Jesus, right?!

Your prayers would be aligned with God's will!
- Your sense of purpose would reflect the call of Christ!
  - and with God's help,
  - your life would produce lasting fruit!

My Life Purpose

It was pretty cool to see my friend Jeremiah last week ~
- Because as I've considered my life purpose,
    - and as I've reflected on God's call for my life,
    - I've discovered that I feel like I'm at the center of God's call,
    - when I get to see God's, fruit grow in the life of another (like with Jeremiah) ...

Perhaps this is because the Call to Be Fruitful
- <u>is centered on Christ's command -- to love each other</u>
    - For when we are connected in authentic relationships,
    - loving and serving one another,
    - then God's spiritual fruit grows in us!

After all,
- According to Jesus, loving one another is not optional for his disciples ~
- Jesus repeated what he said in verse 12 again in verse 17,
    "THIS IS MY COMMAND: LOVE EACH OTHER"

Brothers and sisters in Christ,
- We're not called to just tolerate or be nice to one another...
- We're not called to just create some kind of fake warm-fuzzy feeling in the room...
- The kind of love that Jesus commands,
    - is the kind of love HE has for US...?
- I once heard this Jesus-kind of love described as
    "the indomitable determination to seek the maximum benefit of the other person."

And as we noted earlier, Jesus said that the ultimate expression of this others-centered love
- is to lay down your life for your friends ~
    - For while we were still sinners,
        - Christ died for us...
        - His body was broken...
        - His blood was shed for us...

- That's how much GOD loves you ~
    - The Father gave up his one and only Son,
    - so that all who believe in Him,
    - and remain in Him,
    - will not wither away like a dead branch thrown in the fire,
    - but will have eternal life with God forever
- We will remain connected to the vine,
    - and will forever grow in Christ-likeness ~

This is your Life Purpose!

So, <u>Continue in Christ's love,</u>

    <u>and discover God's call...</u>

        <u>...to a fruitful life</u> – to God be the glory!

Let's Pray...

Dear Jesus,

We come to you with a common desire. We want to experience the complete joy of an abiding relationship with you, and we want to share the wonder of a fruitful life with others. We pray that You will dwell in our hearts, and that your love will overflow in our relationships, so that people will know You and lives will be changed for eternity. We pray these things in Jesus' name, Amen.

REFLECT and RESPOND (Questions for personal or group reflection):

- Read today's Bible passage. How is the Holy Spirit speaking to you?

- When have you experienced God's pruning for greater fruitfulness?

- How do you ensure a lively relational connection with Jesus?

- How fruitful would your life be if you were isolated from Jesus and others?

- Why is it significant that Jesus chose you to be fruitful?

- How will you remain committed to your life purpose of loving God and others?

Your Unique Vocational Call

Part 7 of My Life Purpose: How to Discover God's Call

Ephesians 4:1-16

> Focus Statement: There are three levels of your unique vocational call.
>
> Function Statement: Passionately pursue the call of Christ and discover your life purpose!

Scripture Reading Ephesians 4:1-16 (NLT)

¹ Therefore I, a prisoner for serving the Lord, beg you to lead a life worthy of your calling, for you have been called by God. ² Always be humble and gentle. Be patient with each other, making allowance for each other's faults because of your love. ³ Make every effort to keep yourselves united in the Spirit, binding yourselves together with peace. ⁴ For there is one body and one Spirit, just as you have been called to one glorious hope for the future.

⁵ There is one Lord, one faith, one baptism,
⁶ one God and Father of all,
who is over all, in all, and living through all.

⁷ However, he has given each one of us a special gift through the generosity of Christ.
⁸ That is why the Scriptures say,

> *"When he ascended to the heights,*
> *he led a crowd of captives*
> *and gave gifts to his people."*

⁹ Notice that it says, "he ascended." This clearly means that Christ also descended to our lowly world. ¹⁰ And the same one who descended is the one who ascended higher than all the heavens, so that he might fill the entire universe with himself.

¹¹ Now these are the gifts Christ gave to the church: the apostles, the prophets, the evangelists, and the pastors and teachers. ¹² Their responsibility is to equip God's people to do his work and build up the church, the body of Christ. ¹³ This will continue until we all come to such unity in our faith and knowledge of God's Son that we will be mature in the Lord, measuring up to the full and complete standard of Christ.

¹⁴ Then we will no longer be immature like children. We won't be tossed and blown about by every wind of new teaching. We will not be influenced when people try to trick us with lies so clever, they sound like the truth. ¹⁵ Instead, we will speak the truth in love, growing in every way more and more like Christ, who is the head of his body, the church. ¹⁶ He makes the whole body fit together perfectly. As each part does its own special work, it helps the other parts grow, so that the whole body is healthy and growing and full of love.

MESSAGE

Let's pray...

Heavenly Father, we thank you for the gift of your Holy Word. Open our ears and our hearts, Lord, to the life-changing power of your Word, and cause it to transform our lives, making us more like Jesus, in whose name we pray. Amen.

Today is Part 7 in our series on "My Life's Purpose",

- and while over the past 5 weeks, we have covered Five Facets of God's Call,
    - including The Call to Follow
    - The Call to Faith
    - The Call to Fellowship,
    - The Call to a Special Function,
    - And The Call to Be Fruitful,
- our focus today is on "**Your Unique Vocational Call**"

In other words,

- we are talking about

1. God's Call and **You**

The Apostle Paul states it clearly in verse 1,

- "You have been called by God"

    - The question is ~
        - Do you know what that means?
        - Do you understand what your Unique Vocational Call is?
        - Are you aware of your Life Purpose?

    - Midland students ~
        - by a show of hands,
        - How many of you know what God's Call is for your life?

    - Church family ~ how about you?
        - How many of you know what your Life Purpose is?

I truly believe God has a unique purpose and a special work for each of us to do,

- And yet some people never fully discover what their purpose is ~
    - Maybe because they've never really considered it...
    - or maybe because they haven't learned what God says about it in the Bible...

And so that's our goal today ~
- to explore what God's Word says about God's Call and You ~
    - so that you may be better equipped to discover your life purpose...

In Ephesians 4, Paul made several definitive statements about the nature of God's call ~
- And the Greek word that he used for "call" or "calling" is the noun, *kleesis*,
    - which is related to the verb, *kaleo*, "to call",
    - and is used in the New Testament,
        - **only of callings *issued by God***

You see,
- For Paul,
    - to be called by God out of the world,
        - and into the body of Christ,
        - is the highest vocation possible ~?

The King James Version translates verse one,

"Walk worthy of the *vocation* wherewith ye are called"

Or as the New Living Translation says,
- "Lead a life worthy of your calling" (v. 1-4)

Of course,
- Paul is not saying that we are called by God *because we are worthy*
    - for the calling by which we are made the children of God is utterly gracious ~
- But, after God calls us to be part of the Body of Christ,
    (and in response to that unspeakable gift)

- we should endeavor to do everything in our power,
- to live lives that are *worthy* of our calling...

And as Paul says in verse 2,

- that means being "**humble** and **gentle**"...
- and being "**patient** with each other,
    - making allowances for each other's faults,
    - because of our **love**..."

There is a clear sense, then,
- that a big part of our vocation,
- and of God's call on our lives,
    - has to do with how we relate with one another ~

For God's purpose is that we would "maintain the **unity** of the Spirit"
- and "bind ourselves together with **peace**" (v. 3)

After all, as Paul adds in verse 4,
- "There is **one body**"
- "and **one Spirit**"
- "just as (we) have been called to **one glorious hope** for the future"

And so, God's purpose for us – as The Church – is that we would **be ONE** ~
- For as Paul adds in verse 5,
- "There is **one** Lord,
    - **one** faith,
    - **one** baptism,
    - **one** God and Father of all"

Still, unity in the body of Christ is not about uniformity ~
- and personal uniqueness is not to be suppressed...

Yes, we are one body, with Jesus as the head ~
- <u>Yet, God has given each of us special gifts</u> (v. 5-11)

- And therefore, we each have a unique vocational call ~
    - We each have a part to play...

  As we discussed a couple weeks ago, in Romans 12,
    - The body of Christ is made up of many parts,
        - each with a special function...

  For we have a variety of gifts, functions, and roles to play ~
    - Some are teachers,
        - others have the gift of hospitality...
    - Some are evangelists,
        - others have the gift of administration...
    - Some are pastors,
        - others are sent as missionaries...
    - Some are gifted for leadership,
        - Others are called to serve behind the scenes...

  By design, a variety of gifts are given ~
  - And it takes all of us together,
    - with each one of us doing our part,
    - to experience the fullness of God's call ~

- Therefore, <u>your responsibility is to use your gifts to do God's work</u> (v. 12-16)
  - for as verse 12 says (of church leaders – like pastors and teachers),
  - "their responsibility is **to *equip God's people* to do his work,**
    and build up the church, the body of Christ"

So, what about you?
  - How are you using your gifts to do God's work?
  - How and what are you giving to God?
  - What would it mean for you to give God your "first fruits"?
    - and the best of your gifts?
  - What would it mean for you to discover and fully live out your life purpose?!

My Life Purpose

During my sabbatical this summer,
- I spent some time with my younger brother, Matt, who is also a pastor
- He serves a church in Sierra Vista, Arizona,
    - a military town near the Fort Huachuca Army base
- A few months ago,
    - His church "adopted" a small, 40-member church without a pastor,
        - in a town a few miles away,
        - helping to revitalize the struggling congregation
- At my brother's church,
    - They have a team of "lay speakers",
        - who rotate giving messages at the smaller sister church
    - And it seemed like the partnership was really beginning to bear fruit~
        - there was energy and joy in the worship,
        - and the Holy Spirit really seemed to be at work…
    - It was kind of like the Church in Ephesians 4,
        - With each person using their gifts to build up the church…

Until about 3 weeks ago,
- When, at 6:15 p.m. on a Thursday night, when no one was at the church,
- an arsonist intentionally set fire to the church building in five different places,
- and burned the building down to the ground – a complete and total loss…

It was a devastating event – an evil act meant to destroy a Church…

But you know what?
- It didn't destroy the Church.
- Yes, the building was gone,
    - But the people, and their love for God and one another, are growing stronger,
    - And the Lord is providing new ways for people to step up and use their gifts

My Life Purpose

You see, sometimes God works through our struggles to reveal His purposes…

Sometimes, when we are stretched beyond what we think we can bear,
- and we begin to fully rely on the Lord,
- and offer all of what we have to God,
    - and commit our hearts and our gifts and our resources to God's work,
    - THEN we discover our purpose…

So… What will it take in your life?

- What old habits, or old ways of thinking, need to be burned away?

- What will it take for you to hear and respond to God's call?

(I hope and pray it doesn't take a tragic loss…)

Instead, I hope to offer you 3 statements of purpose that you can claim for yourself today ~
- And that can help you discover and live out God's call for your life…

So here they are – think of these as
2. <u>Three Levels of Your Unique Vocational Call</u>
    - And the first is this:
    - **"I am called to Jesus"**
        - Repeat that with me: ("I am called to Jesus")
            - You see, that's our primary call, and it **never changes**
            - Jesus calls us to Himself…
            - He calls us to follow him…
                - and learn from him…
            - He calls us to trust him,
                - and love him.

My Life Purpose

- Jesus said to his soon-to-be disciples,
    - "Come, follow me, and I will teach you to fish for people",
    - And they discovered their life purpose...

- Jesus looked at the rich man who had kept all of God's commandments,
    - yet was still seeking to find his life purpose,
    - and feeling genuine love for him,
    - Jesus told him,

        "There is still one thing you haven't done.
        Go and sell all your possessions and give the money to the poor,
        and you will have treasure in heaven.
        Then come, follow me."

The call to Jesus is the first level of Your Unique Vocational Call
- Have you heard his invitation?
- Have you listened?
- How have you responded?
- What do you need to let go of, to be free to say, "I am called to Jesus"?

You see, no matter what else happens in your life,
- When you say "YES" to the call to Jesus,
    - You are a beloved child of God,
        - and an indispensable part of the Body of Christ,
        - and nothing – and no one – can ever take that away ~
            - So, claim this never-changing purpose,
            - And say "Yes, I am called to Jesus!"

The second level of your Unique Vocational Call is this:
- **"I am called to become more like Jesus"**

    - Repeat this one with me, too: ("I am called to become more like Jesus")

    You see, not only are we called to Jesus – we are called to become *more like Him*
    - and this process of transformation is **lifelong and ongoing**

I think that's what Paul was talking about, when he said in verse 14 and 15,

> "Then we will no longer be immature like children.
> We won't be tossed and blown about by every wind of new teaching.
> We will not be influenced when people try to trick us with lies so clever, they sound like the truth.
> Instead, we will **speak the truth in love**,
> **growing in every way more and more like Christ**,
> who is the head of his body, the church."

And in Romans 12, Paul urges us,

> "Don't copy the behavior and customs of this world,
> **but let God transform you into a new person**
> **by changing the way you think.**
> **Then you will learn to know God's will for you,**
> which is good and pleasing and perfect.

And to the Thessalonians, Paul proclaimed,

> "God has called us to live **holy lives**, not impure lives." (4:7)

Of course, living like Jesus is not easy ~

As 1 Peter 2:21 says,

> "For God called you to do good,
> **even if it means suffering**,
> just as Christ suffered for you.
> He is your example, and **you must follow in his steps**."

And so, you see, your journey of becoming more like Jesus is lifelong and ongoing,
- and your journey probably looks different than the person next to you,
- but never-the-less, we can all claim the 2nd level as part of our life purpose:

    "I am called to become more like Jesus" ...

The third level of Your Unique Vocational Call is this (and let's say it together):
- **"I am called to use my gifts in service to God and others"**

    - And while this call also never changes,

    what this looks like in your life, **may change over time...**

- This is what Ephesians 4, and Romans 12, and 1 Corinthians 12 are all about ~
    - The call to use the gifts God gives you in service to God and others ~
        - For there may be seasons when God calls you to use your gift of hospitality to welcome or care for a stranger…
        - There may be times when God calls you to use your administrative gifts to help launch a new ministry, or assist a neighbor through a difficult loss…
        - There may be a financial need, and God calls you to use your gift of generosity and faithfulness to help…
        - There may be a season when you are called to use all your gifts in service to our country…

    - The needs around you,
        - and opportunities that God gives you, may change over time ~
        - Doors may open – and doors may close…

    - But you and I can always claim the third level as our purpose:

        "I am called to use my gifts in service to God and others"

And as we do, then Paul's statement in verse 16 becomes a reality ~

Paul says,

> **"(Christ) makes the whole body fit together perfectly.**
> **As each part does its own special work, it helps the other parts grow,**
> **so that the whole body is healthy and growing and full of love."**

THAT's our purpose!
- We are called and gifted by the Holy Spirit to participate in the ministry of Christ!

R.C. Sproul put it this way:
> "Every person in the body of Christ has a significant task to perform.
> No-one is insignificant; no-one is unimportant.

There is no such thing as a misfit in the body of Christ because Christ himself, the head of the body, is the one who makes sure that we fit together and knit together into the unity of his body.[1]

And so, Church –

Give it all you've got!

Passionately pursue the call of Christ –

- Claim the three levels of Your Unique Vocation Call as your own ~
    - "I am called to Jesus"
    - "I am called to become more like Jesus" and
    - "I am called to use my gifts in service to God and others"

Do this,

- and discover your life purpose!

Amen? Amen!

Let's pray…

Lord Jesus, we claim your purpose for our lives. Thank you for calling us to Jesus. Make us more and more like Him. Guide us and lead us in using the gifts you give us, to serve your purposes. Transform us into people who walk in your will, as we follow Your way of love. We pray this in Jesus' name, Amen.

---

[1] Sproul, R. C. (1994). *The Purpose of God: Ephesians* (pp. 107–108). Scotland: Christian Focus Publications.

REFLECT and RESPOND (Questions for personal or group reflection):

- Read today's Bible passage. How is the Holy Spirit speaking to you?

- What does Paul say is the common bond among the Ephesians?

- What makes each person unique?

- According to Ephesians 4, what is the goal of the church?

- How have you responded to God's call?

- In what ways are you using your gifts to do God's work?

A Hope-Filled Formula
Part 8 of *My Life Purpose: How to Discover God's Call*

Romans 8:18-39

> Focus Statement: NEED + GIFTS + HUNGER = GOD'S CALL
>
> Function Statement: Passionately pursue the call of Christ and change lives!

Scripture Reading   Romans 8:18-39 (NLT)

18 Yet what we suffer now is nothing compared to the glory he will reveal to us later. 19 For all creation is waiting eagerly for that future day when God will reveal who his children really are. 20 Against its will, all creation was subjected to God's curse. But with eager hope, 21 the creation looks forward to the day when it will join God's children in glorious freedom from death and decay. 22 For we know that all creation has been groaning as in the pains of childbirth right up to the present time. 23 And we believers also groan, even though we have the Holy Spirit within us as a foretaste of future glory, for we long for our bodies to be released from sin and suffering. We, too, wait with eager hope for the day when God will give us our full rights as his adopted children, including the new bodies he has promised us. 24 We were given this hope when we were saved. (If we already have something, we don't need to hope for it. 25 But if we look forward to something we don't yet have, we must wait patiently and confidently.)

26 And the Holy Spirit helps us in our weakness. For example, we don't know what God wants us to pray for. But the Holy Spirit prays for us with groanings that cannot be expressed in words. 27 And the Father who knows all hearts knows what the Spirit is saying, for the Spirit pleads for us believers in harmony with God's own will. 28 And we know that God causes everything to work together for the good of those who love God and are called according to his purpose for them. 29 For God knew his people in advance, and he chose them to become like his Son, so that his Son would be the firstborn among many brothers and sisters. 30 And having chosen them, he called them to come to him. And having called them, he gave them right standing with himself. And having given them right standing, he gave them his glory.

31 What shall we say about such wonderful things as these? If God is for us, who can ever be against us? 32 Since he did not spare even his own Son but gave him up for us all, won't he also give us everything else? 33 Who dares accuse us whom God has chosen for his own? No one—for God himself has given us right standing with himself. 34 Who then will condemn us? No one—for Christ Jesus died for us and was raised to life for us, and he is sitting in the place of honor at God's right hand, pleading for us.

35 Can anything ever separate us from Christ's love? Does it mean he no longer loves us if we have trouble or calamity, or are persecuted, or hungry, or destitute, or in danger, or threatened with death? 36 (As the Scriptures say, "For your sake we are killed every day; we *are being slaughtered like sheep.") **37** No, despite all these things, overwhelming victory is ours through Christ, who loved us.*

***38** And I am convinced that nothing can ever separate us from God's love. Neither death nor life, neither angels nor demons, neither our fears for today nor our worries about tomorrow—not even the powers of hell can separate us from God's love. **39** No power in the sky above or in the earth below—indeed, nothing in all creation will ever be able to separate us from the love of God that is revealed in Christ Jesus our Lord.*

MESSAGE

Let's pray...
Heavenly Father, thank you for loving us without end. Speak into our hearts this morning, Lord, and empower us to live for you. Give me your words to speak, God, for my words alone are empty apart from your Spirit. In Jesus' name, Amen.

A man decides that his "calling" is to join the circus ~

- He shows up to demonstrate his skills to the impresario...

"I have the most unusual act," he announces. "I'm sure it will amaze you."

He climbs up to the high wire and jumps off!

- He flaps his arms wildly, and finally his fall slows...
- He soars upward, turns, and swoops back again...
- Finally, he stops in mid-air –
    - and gently lowers himself to the ground...

The impresario says,

"Is that all you've got? Bird impressions?"

What's your "calling"?

- What's your life purpose?
- Do you have it figured out?
- Are you living it?!

My Life Purpose

During this series, we've been exploring the various facets of God's Call ~

In many ways,

- we've been on a journey –
- we've been exploring what the Bible says about the Path to Purpose in our lives...
  - And today is no different ~
    - Today we're digging in to Romans 8 –
      - with an ear to what Paul says about God's call for the way we are to live ~

And from the opening verses,

1. We see that part of our Path to Purpose involves **suffering, death and decay...**

- For We live in world filled with needs (v. 18-22)
  - And this has been the case ever since The Fall of mankind in Genesis,
    - when we became subject to God's curse,
    - as a consequence for our disobedience...
  - Paul says in verse 22 that

    "all creation has been groaning, as in the pains of childbirth..."

  - In other words,
    - Ever since we fell into sin,
      - we have been on a path filled with pain ~
      - for we are lost and hopeless apart from God...
      - we have all sinned and fallen short of God's glorious ideal...
      - we all need forgiveness and grace...
    - And there's nothing we can do –
      - on our own – to resolve this need ~

Thankfully, Paul offers tremendous hope ~

- For although we suffer and groan,

  "we have the Holy Spirit within us as a foretaste of future glory" (v. 23)

This means our path does not end in pain ~
- We have a higher calling ~
  - a greater purpose ~
- Therefore, <u>as God's children, we long to relieve suffering</u> (v. 23-25)
  - We long for the day when sin and suffering are no more ~
  - and all creation joins "God's children in glorious freedom from death and decay" (v. 21)

  - As Paul says in verse 23,
    "we long for our bodies to be released from sin and suffering" ... and
    "we wait with eager hope for the day God will give us our full rights
      as his adopted children, including the new bodies he has promised us"!

So, what about you?
- Are you excited for the day you get a new resurrection body?!
- Are you eagerly awaiting the day, when Jesus returns, and makes all things new?!

Or...

Are you just tired and weary?
- Do you feel weak and worn out?
- Have you lost sight of God's greater purpose and plan?...

It's understandable if you have ~
- Because it's easy to feel overwhelmed by the suffering in the world ~
  - whether it's the destruction of wildfires and mass shootings...
  - or the division of politics and prejudice...
    - we live in a world that is broken and weary...

But we are not alone ~
- As Paul writes in verse 26,
- "The Holy Spirit helps us in our weakness" (v. 26-27)
    - And then Paul gives an example ~
        - You see, even "when we don't know what God wants us to pray for," Paul says,
        - the "Holy Spirit prays for us with groanings that cannot be expressed in words"
    - And Our Heavenly Father understands what the Spirit is saying,
        - because God knows our hearts,
        - and the Spirit "pleads for us believers in harmony with God's own will" (v. 27)

This means that even when we are tired, weary, and broken,
- The Spirit intercedes for us,
    - in alignment with God's purposes...

And as a result,
- "God causes everything to work together for the good of those who love God,
    - and who are called according to **his purpose** for them" (v. 28)
        - This doesn't mean our life will be "smooth sailing" and "problem-free",
            - but it does mean God is looking out for us ~
            - and that God has a plan and a purpose for our lives
    - Specifically,
        - Paul says that God's plan involves a process of making us more like Jesus ~
            - For not only are we chosen "to become like his Son",
            - but we are also called to "come to him",
            - and to be given right standing with God, to the glory of God!
    - In this way,
        - God is at work through all our life circumstances,
            - to shape us more into the likeness of Jesus...
        - Sometimes that involves suffering and hardship...
        - Sometimes it means learning tough lessons the hard way...

But one thing is certain ~
- Through it all,
  - through all the ups and downs,
  - through all the twists and turns,
    - God has our back!

Like our Huskers, we might be winless through the first half of the season,
- and things might look pretty bleak ~
  - But all is not lost ~
    - We need to trust the process...
    - For God is at work, reshaping us...
  - There might be days when we have a hard time seeing the Master Plan,
    - But that doesn't mean God has forgotten us ~
      - For God is working all things together for our good ~
      - and there's no better place to be, if you think about it...

For as Paul proclaimed,

"If God is for us, who can ever be against us?"! (v. 31)

Besides... Paul adds,

"Since God did not even spare his own Son, but gave him up for us all,

won't he also give us everything else?" (v. 32)

You see – the beauty of being called by God – is that Christ has already won victory for us!
- Jesus defeated sin and death!
- The battle is over!
- His unstoppable love never ends!
- This means <u>NOTHING can ever separate us from God's love in Christ</u> (v. 31-39)
  - No sin
  - No shame
  - No past
  - No pain
    - can separate you from God's love!

- No height
- No depth
- No fear
- No death
    - can separate you from God's love!

And so even when we may not feel like it ~
- God's love for us is unrelenting ~
    - His love and faithfulness endure forever ~
    - and the Lord is working all things together for our good,
    - when we Love God,
    - and are called according to His purposes!

But there's still one BIG QUESTION ~
- How do we discern what God's Call is?
- How do we know whether something is God's Call, or Not?

I've wrestled with this question a lot over the course of my life...
- I've sought wisdom from mentors, seminary professors, and trusted Christian friends...
- and in the process,
3. I've found a Hope-Filled Formula to be very helpful,
    - when it comes to discerning God's Call ~

And here it is:

NEED + GIFTS + HUNGER = GOD'S CALL

So, allow me to explain...

The formula starts with a **NEED** ~
- meaning there's some issue - or opportunity that emerges,
- some void - or problem that exists...
    - and you become aware of it

My Life Purpose

Maybe it's a friend who's hurting...
- Maybe it's a stranger in need of help...
- Maybe it's a new career path...
- Maybe it's a financial need...
    - a relational need...
    - or a societal need...

Whatever the case may be,
- you become aware of a NEED,
    - and you then ask yourself,
        - do I have **GIFTS** or **RESOURCES** that can help with this NEED?

In other words,
- Has God given me the capacity to do something about this NEED?
    - Do my gifts match up with the need?
        - If not, then it's probably not something God is calling you to be a part of ~
            - (of course, it could be that you know someone who does have the gifts or resources that match the need, and your role is to share the need with that other person)
        - But – if your gifts DO match the need,
            - if you have access to the resources required to address the need,
            - then it's time to consider your degree of **HUNGER** or inner drive ~
                - meaning, "are you motivated to use your gifts to meet the need?"
            - Has God stirred a spiritual hunger within you, to take action?
                - Has the Holy Spirit sparked a desire within you?
                    - to use your gifts to address the need?
    - If so... if you DO sense an inner HUNGER to use your GIFTS to meet the NEED,
        - if all three elements of the formula are there,
        - then it may very well be God's Call ~

However, if any one of the three factors is missing,
- then it's likely not God's Call for you at this time ~

You see, it's probably NOT God's call,
- if you see a NEED, and you have the GIFTS, but don't have any HUNGER to use them…
- or if you see a NEED and are HUNGRY to take action, but you lack the necessary GIFTS…
- or if you have certain GIFTS and the HUNGER to use them,
    - but there's no current NEED or OPPORTUNITY to apply them ~

Whichever the case may be, if any one factor is missing, it's likely not God's call at this time ~

However,
- If all three factors are present –
    - If you see a NEED,
    - and you have the GIFTS or RESOURCES it takes to help,
    - and God gives you the spiritual HUNGER to act,
        - then there's a good chance God may be calling you to do so!

The late Ty Schenzel, founder of the Hope Center for Kids, used to ask the question, "What's YOUR problem?"

Meaning, what issue – or need – or situation weighs on you,
- to the point that God calls you to do something about it?

For Ty, his "problem" was hopelessness in so many of today's youth ~
- especially African American kids living in North Omaha…
- The NEED -- was kids living in hopelessness –
    - and therefore, for those kids -- consequences meant nothing…
- And so, 20 years ago, God called Ty to start the Hope Center for Kids, in North Omaha ~
    - and then about 5 years ago,
    - our church began working with Ty to launch Hope Fremont

My Life Purpose

Today,
- both locations offer a safe place where kids are inspired with the HOPE of God's love,
  - and they are equipped to identify and use their gifts to make a difference

We learned this morning about a NEED for adult mentors at Hope Fremont
- And I encourage you to consider if you have the gifts and desire to mentor a kid
- Because I know that if God calls some of you to serve as Mentors,
  - the experience will change lives...

Just this week,
- our church once again hosted the Hope Fremont Thanksgiving Dinner Family Night
- And this time, we not only fed a couple hundred kids and parents a delicious dinner,
- our Deacons also donated 5 gift certificates for Christmas Dinner SHARE Food Boxes,
  - which we raffled off ~

And I have to tell you, it was so awesome ~
- as we called out the raffle ticket winning numbers, and each family came forward,
- The first winner, got tears in her eyes, when she realized we were giving her family a food box with a ham, and everything needed to make a full Christmas dinner,
  - she smiled wide and said, "thank you!", and asked if she could give us a hug ~
- And then the 2nd winner, who witnessed how thankful the first winner was,
  - asked if she could donate her box to another family in need ~
- It was such a beautiful moment ~
  - all made possible because Ty Schenzel answered God's call 20 years ago...
- And our church family answered God's call 5 years ago,
  - and again, this week,
  - to offer HOPE to those who are living in hopelessness...

"God causes everything to work together for the good of those who love God and are called according to his purpose for them." (v. 28)

My Life Purpose

What about you?
- Will you answer God's call?
- Will you apply the "Hope-filled formula" in your life to guide you?
- Will you offer your gifts to help fulfill God's purposes?

I hope and pray the answer is "YES!"
- I hope all of us are ready and willing to passionately pursue the Call of Christ ~

4. And to help us follow the Path to Purpose, let's review the <u>Next Steps:</u>
   - First, <u>Pray for God to open your eyes to NEEDS</u>
     - If you are seeking to discern God's Call,
       - start by asking the Lord to lay a NEED on your heart
     - We know the world is filled with needs ~
       - And so, the question is, which need is God calling you to respond to?

Once you have a NEED in mind, the second step is to
- <u>Consider how God could use your GIFTS</u> in response to that need
  - Remember that it's GOD who works all things together for good,
    - It's not YOUR responsibility to fix the problem,
    - or meet the need, all by yourself...
  - The question is,
    - How could GOD use your GIFTS to help address the need?

Finally, the third step is to
- <u>Discern your degree of Holy Spirit HUNGER</u> ~
  - In other words, is the Spirit moving you to take action?
    - Remember, the Spirit helps us in our weakness ~
    - Yet, when God stirs in your heart,
      - it's up to you how you respond ~
    - You can welcome the Spirit's leading, and follow God's call...
      - or you can make the selfish choice, and go your own way...

So, what's it going to be, for you?...

God is calling you to passionately pursue the call of Christ -- and change lives!
- Will you follow God's call?
- Will you dedicate your gifts -- and offer your life -- to the Lord?

Will you discover your life purpose –
- and share the unstoppable, never-ending love of Jesus with a world in need?

I believe that is God's Call for all of us ~
- to live hope-filled lives of purpose ~
- because everyone NEEDS to know they are created in God's image,
- with a unique mix of GIFTS and abilities,
- that the Spirit PLEADS for us to use for good – and for God's glory.

So, Let's Go for It.

Amen? Amen.

Let's pray...

Heavenly Father, we offer our lives to you today – and we pray your Spirit would guide us in using the gifts you've blessed us with to change lives. Transform our hearts on the journey, O God, to become more like Jesus, as we follow Your way of love. We pray this in Jesus' name, Amen.

REFLECT and RESPOND (Questions for personal or group reflection):

- Read today's Bible passage. How is the Holy Spirit speaking to you?

- What needs in the world weigh on you or tug at your heart?

- What spiritual gifts and abilities has God blessed you with?

- How could the Spirit work through your gifts to relieve or resolve a need?

- Why are all three factors of the formula vital to discerning God's call?

- What is the outcome when we live according to God's purpose for our lives?

How to Discover God's Call
Part 9 of *My Life Purpose: How to Discover God's Call*

John 10:1-10

> Focus Statement: Follow Jesus and live abundantly.
>
> Function Statement: Follow the call of Christ and discover your life purpose!

Scripture Reading   John 10:1-10 (ESV)

¹ "Truly, truly, I say to you, he who does not enter the sheepfold by the door but climbs in by another way, that man is a thief and a robber. ² But he who enters by the door is the shepherd of the sheep. ³ To him the gatekeeper opens. The sheep hear his voice, and he calls his own sheep by name and leads them out. ⁴ When he has brought out all his own, he goes before them, and the sheep follow him, for they know his voice. ⁵ A stranger they will not follow, but they will flee from him, for they do not know the voice of strangers." ⁶ This figure of speech Jesus used with them, but they did not understand what he was saying to them.

⁷ So Jesus again said to them, "Truly, truly, I say to you, I am the door of the sheep. ⁸ All who came before me are thieves and robbers, but the sheep did not listen to them. ⁹ I am the door. If anyone enters by me, he will be saved and will go in and out and find pasture. ¹⁰ The thief comes only to steal and kill and destroy. I came that they may have life and have it abundantly.

MESSAGE

Let's pray...

Lord, Jesus. We desire to hear from You today. Teach us what it is that you would have us learn, and how it is that you would have us live. Lord, give me your words to speak, and open our hearts and minds to your ways. In Jesus' name, Amen.

There once was a baby camel who asked his mother,
"Mom, why do I have these huge three-toed feet?"

His mother replied,
"Well, son, your toes help you stay on top of the soft sand when we trek across the desert."

A few minutes later the baby camel asked, "Mom, why do I have these long eyelashes?"

My Life Purpose

His mother replied,

"Well, son, your eyelashes help keep the sand out of your eyes on our trips through the desert."

A few minutes later the baby camel asked,
"Mom, why do I have these great big humps on my back?"

His mother, who was getting a little impatient with her son, replied,
"Well, son, your humps store water for our long treks across the desert,
so you can go without drinking for long periods of time."

"That's great, Mom," the baby camel said.
"We have huge feet to stop us from sinking, long eyelashes to keep sand out of our eyes, and humps to store water. But...Mom?"

"Yes, son?"

"Why are we in the zoo??"

Are you living life the way it was meant to be lived?
- Are you fulfilling your life purpose?
- or does it feel like you're missing out on something?

Are you experiencing the fullness of the real and abundant life that Jesus has to offer?
- or are you settling for a false sense of reality?

Are you doing what God created you to do?
- Are you living the life God created you to live?

Maybe you feel a little like the camel in the zoo.
- Life is relatively easy... things are going along pretty smoothly...
- but you have a nagging feeling inside,
- that maybe you aren't living up to your God-given potential –
- that there is something more out there ~

Living in a zoo isn't all bad, but it's certainly not what camels were created to do.

My Life Purpose

Living outside the will of God may not be all bad, either,
- but it's not what you were created to do.

And so today we look to Jesus to help us learn how to discover God's call ~
- and to experience the "abundant life" we are called to live ~

It's a life of adventure!
- It's a life of significance!
- It's a life worth living!

In John 10,
- Jesus tells a story to some Jews and Pharisees about ordinary, everyday Sheep…

And it makes sense that Jesus chose Sheep to illustrate his message ~
- For sheep were a common part of life for the Jewish people --
    - some of his listeners were undoubtedly shepherds
- And sheep had also been a common part of the Jewish religious culture as well ~
    - We think of the fatted calf offered as a sacrifice…
    - or the Shepherd-boy David,
        - and his use of sheep and shepherd imagery in the Psalms…

But sheep aren't so much a part of our lives today ~
- And so perhaps we might benefit from a little "sheep-education" --
1. So, let's talk <u>a Little About Sheep</u> ~
    - First of all, <u>they live in **flocks** and **folds**</u>

        - A FLOCK is a group of sheep that belong to a particular owner ~
            - They spend their lives together as a group,
            - and they naturally herd together in flocks,
            - both for a sense of community,
            - and also as a defense against predators…

        - A FOLD is basically a mixture of 2 or more FLOCKS ~

- A fold occurs when multiple sheep owners decide to "fold" their sheep together,
  - leaving one shepherd to watch the flock,
  - so, the others can be free to go about other business…
- Shepherds might rotate watching the fold for one another…

- A "Sheepfold" also refers to a particular place where the fold of sheep are kept ~
  - It was usually a place with secure boundaries –
    - a fence, a cave, a wall…
    - with just one entrance –
    - so that the one shepherd could keep watch over the fold

Now sometimes, these days, sheep are depicted as "unintelligent" animals ~
- standing around in their flocks or folds kind of clueless…
- But modern scientists have recently discovered that sheep may be smarter
  - than they are typically made out to be ~
- For example, researchers have determined that
  - a sheep can remember up to 50 faces of other sheep for as long as 2 years…
  - Also, sheep have been known to figure out how to get across a "cattle-guard",
    - by rolling on their backs…

And so, it should come as no surprise,
- that sheep are able to recognize and <u>follow THEIR shepherd's voice</u> ~
  - that when their owner comes to the gate of the fold,
  - and calls out their name,
  - that they will respond by following the shepherd's voice,
  - much like a well-trained dog might respond to its master ~
    - "Come here, Fluffy! Come here, Harold! Time to go out to the pasture!"
    - And good ol' Fluffy and Harold would turn,
      - and follow the familiar voice of their shepherd
    - They would follow their shepherd out the main gate of the fold and beyond
  - So even though there may be multiple flocks mixed together in a fold,

- They didn't have to worry too much about tagging the ears of the sheep,
  ◦ or branding them,
- Because the sheep would only respond to the voice of their particular Master

- For sheep <u>won't follow a stranger's voice, but will scatter</u> – and run the other way
  - So...
    Jesus explains,
    ~ anyone who would come to the fold and try to enter by another way,
    ~ other than the main gate, must be a thief...
    ~ They must be up to no good...
    ~ They must be just trying to come and mislead the sheep,
    ~ or steal them altogether....

Of course, Jesus has a point he is trying to make here ~
- and it begins with making the connection that
2. <u>We Are Kinda Like Sheep</u>

For just like the sheep Jesus has been talking about,
- <u>We are created for community</u>
  - We are connected in families, or flocks
  - And in groups of families, or folds
    ◦ Neighborhoods...
    ◦ Schools...
    ◦ Work places...
    ◦ Clubs...
    ◦ Churches...

- And within those flocks and folds, <u>we tend to follow the voices that are familiar to us</u>
  - That's why a newborn child will respond to the voice of its mother,

- - - over the voice of a total stranger...
  - That's why we are more likely to listen to advice from a friend we trust,
    - than from someone we have never met before...
  - In fact, when someone misleads us,
    - we tend to avoid them...

- <u>For we are likely to become scattered when we are misled</u> or deceived ~
  - Our fur gets a little ruffled...
  - We feel shaken and confused...
  - And may become anxious or fearful of the unknown...

Like a sheep led astray,
- we long for the familiar once again...
  - we long to hear the voice of goodness and truth and love...
- we seek out the voice of someone we can trust...

That's why being connected in a church family is so important ~
- because it's one place where we can feel safe in the fold ~

- As we learn to trust one another,
  - and know that we have a Shepherd who's watching over us,
  - we discover that we are not alone,
    - but that we are in this together...

- And we learn to hear the voice of the Lord speaking into our lives ~
  - A familiar voice...
    - A strong voice...
    - A wise voice...
- For like sheep,
  - we are created to be in community –
  - and we long for the Shepherd's voice, saying:

My Life Purpose

- ○ "Come, Follow Me. Let's go on an adventure together."

And that's really where a Life of Purpose begins ~

- That's <u>How we Discover God's Call</u> ~
    - ○ it starts by recognizing the Lord's loving voice,
    - ○ and opening the door of your heart to Jesus…

Because when you hear the Lord call you by name,

- <u>and you enter by "The Door",</u>
    - – <u>you receive three gifts: 1) salvation, 2) freedom and 3) purpose</u>

As Jesus said in verse 9,

- – "I am the door."
- – "If anyone enters by me, he will be saved, and will go in and out, and find pasture"

You see, when pass through the **Door of salvation**,

- – The Good Shepherd delivers us from evil,
    - ○ and saves us from suffering eternal punishment for our sins…
- – Because when Jesus Christ was crucified on the cross,
    - ○ and his blood marked the door to life ~
    - ○ He not only paid the price for our sins…
    - ○ He defeated sin and death,
        - ~ by rising from the grave!

- – And so, by entering through the Door and trusting in Him,
    - ○ by responding to His voice calling our name,
    - ○ We discover God's call to salvation!

- – The second gift we receive from Jesus is the **door of freedom**
    - ○ Jesus says that all who enter by Him,
        - ~ will have the freedom to go in and out as they please
    - ○ So, when we become a follower of Christ, we are no longer a slave to sin
        - ~ But we are set free in Christ

My Life Purpose

- ◦ We receive a freedom from guilt and shame,
    - ~ The weight of our failures is lifted!
    - ~ We are given a second chance!
    - ~ We become a new creation in Christ!
    - ~ Free to live the abundant life that Jesus has to offer!
    - ~ Unrestrained by our burdens!
    - ~ Unhampered by our sin!

- ◦ For when the Son sets us free,
    - ~ we are free indeed!   (John 8:36)

Still, in some ways, this call to freedom can be risky ~

– because God has given us the freedom to choose…
- ◦ And so, we can choose to follow and obey the voice of the Lord,
    - ~ **OR** we can choose to follow the voices of this world…

But when we listen to the voice of the Good Shepherd,

and enter through the Door, we also receive a third gift: **We find purpose**

- Not only are we saved…
- And not only do we find freedom…
- But Jesus says we also find "pasture" ~
    - o the Greek here literally means "grazing"

Having discovered God's call to salvation and freedom in Christ,

- we enjoy "grazing" on the fruit of the Spirit ~
- We graze on love, joy, peace, patience, kindness, goodness, faithfulness, gentleness, and self-control…
- We graze on friendship, and laughter, and authentic community…
- We graze on adventure, and truth, and living out our dreams!

In other words,

- We find true joy and purpose and abundant life in Jesus Christ!
- We enjoy genuine love in the community of faith!
- We experience life the way it was meant to be!
- For Jesus came to give the best life possible – abundant life!

But Jesus also said in verse 10 to BEWARE of those who want to deprive you of that ~

- For "The thief comes only to steal and kill and destroy."

And if you think about it,

– We face a lot of "thieves" in our lives ~
  ○ They might be those people who just seem set on messing up our day...
  ○ Those experiences that rob us of our innocence...
  ○ Those temptations that keep us from fully following the Lord...
  ○ Those thoughts that continually trip us up...

– In 1 Peter, the Apostle Peter warns us,

  "Be careful! Watch out for attacks from the devil, your great enemy.

  He prowls around like a roaring lion, looking for some victim to devour." (5:8)

And so "The Thief" that Jesus is talking about in John 10:10 may be the devil himself,
- who is an enemy of God ~?
- and this Thief is in a battle with God for your life ~

For those of you who are passionate followers of Jesus:
- The thief wants to **STEAL** your **JOY**
  ○ The thief wants to take away the joy of life that makes you shine for Christ
  ○ He wants to do whatever it takes to steal your joy from you,
  ○ And replace it with pain, or sorrow, or sadness, or anger, or bitterness...

For those of you who are really trying to learn what it means to truly follow Jesus:

- The thief wants to **KILL** your **WITNESS**
    - The thief wants to trip you up ~
    - He will try to tempt you and distract you away from the truth ~
    - He wants to do whatever it takes to damage your influence for Christ ~
    - And if at all possible,
    - he will try to make you a hypocrite so that you lead others astray as well…

And for those of you who are seeking to know Jesus,

and are just beginning to learn how to follow him:

- The thief wants to **DESTROY** your **LIFE**
    - He wants to wreak havoc and cause unrest ~
    - So that your focus becomes on yourself and your own problems ~
    - Rather than on Jesus

- The thief will try to do whatever it takes to keep you from living for Christ
    - Because the Thief comes only to steal your joy,
        - kill your witness,
        - and destroy your life
    - So, don't listen to his voice ~
    - Don't listen to the voice of the deceiver ~

Instead,

- <u>Follow the voice of Jesus and live abundantly</u>!
- Open The Door to Christ – and Discover God's Call for your life!

Some of you may be familiar with the gameshow, "Let's Make a Deal" ~

- where contestants are given a choice to keep a *known cash prize*
- or trade it for an *unknown prize* behind a door…

Well, some contestants keep the cash in hand,

- and they never open the door…

My Life Purpose

While other contestants return the known prize, and choose a door,
- sometimes the "prize" behind the door is a worthless prank ~
- and sometimes it is a valuable surprise – like a dream vacation or something!

Well, you and I each have a choice to make ~
- we can settle for the things of this world that we "know" and can "see" and "hold",
- or we can choose to open the door to Jesus,
    - and discover an eternal and abundant life with God!

There was a time in my life when I settled.
- I was afraid to open the door.
- I was afraid of the unknown.
- I listened to the voices of the world,
    - and sought meaning and purpose in things other than Christ…
        - whether it was earning good grades in school,
        - doing things just to gain acceptance from others,
        - or chasing after material possessions…

But all of those paths came up empty ~
- They were trap-doors…
- I was lost and alone…
- and couldn't seem to find true fulfillment or purpose in life…

But then, by God's grace, the Lord spoke to me ~
- through the voice of a Pastor who shared the gospel at a college Bible study…
- through the voice of Jen, and other Christian friends who loved and accepted me…
- and through the voice of God revealed in the Bible, and through prayer…

Eventually,
- I heard the Lord call me by name,
    - and I opened the door of my heart to Jesus ~

- - I chose to follow Him…
  - I learned to trust Him…
  - I experienced genuine Christian fellowship and community…
  - I discovered I had gifts for ministry,
    - and a hunger to help others know Jesus,
    - and the abundant life He offers!

- God has been opening (and closing) doors ever since ~
  - and what a joy and honor it is to be on the journey with you!

My hope and prayer is that you would choose to open the door of your heart to the Lord ~
- For Jesus longs to enjoy life with you ~
- and God has an exciting, abundant life in store for you –
  - no matter how old you are,
  - or how long you have known the Lord!

So <u>Follow the call of Christ today – and discover your life purpose!</u>
- Choose "The Door" marked with the love of Jesus,
  - and enjoy the journey!

Let's pray…
Lord Jesus, we thank you for being the Door to eternal and abundant life. We open our hearts to you, Jesus, and welcome you in. We thank you for saving us, and giving us a second chance. We thank you for watching over us, as our Good Shepherd, and for protecting us from evil. Lord, help us to become people who follow you together in love, as we live the abundant life! In Jesus' name, Amen.

My Life Purpose

REFLECT and RESPOND (Questions for personal or group reflection):

- Read today's Bible passage. How is the Holy Spirit speaking to you?

- What "thieves" are out to steal, kill and destroy your life?

- Who is the "shepherd" in this passage, and what is the shepherd's purpose?

- Have you heard the voice of Jesus and entered through "the door"?

- What does this passage teach us about how to discern God's call?

- According to this passage, what is the result of following Jesus?

www.ingramcontent.com/pod-product-compliance
Lightning Source LLC
Chambersburg PA
CBHW081724100526
44591CB00016B/2498